JUSTICE FOR THE POOR

In this study, the author examines the behavior of one group of court-appointed defense attorneys and reaches the conclusion that although, in contrast to popular opinion, these attorneys maintain an adversarial stance against the prosecutors and behave in a legally ethical (or 'procedurally just') manner, case outcomes are unduly shaped by social class and are therefore substantively unjust. This occurs because poor defendants typically lack cultural rhetoric that favorably influences those who construct and operate the criminal court system. Ironically, this indicates that, in many cases, the process of plea bargaining may be more substantively just than trials. A major contribution of the study is the detailed analysis of the manner by which oppression and substantive injustice occur in the adjudication of many cases and how the cultural practices of the powerful can frequently misconstrue, exclude and mute the voices of the poor.

This is dedicated to defenders of the poor everywhere

Justice for the Poor

A Study of Criminal Defense Work

DEBRA S. EMMELMAN
Southern Connecticut State University

ASHGATE

Published by
Ashgate Publishing Limited
Gower House
Croft Road
Aldershot
Hants GU11 3HR
England

Ashgate Publishing Company
Suite 420
101 Cherry Street
Burlington, VT 05401-4405
USA

Ashgate website: http://www.ashgate.com

British Library Cataloguing in Publication Data
Emmelman, Debra S.
    Justice for the poor : a study of criminal defense work. -
    (Law, justice and power)
    1. Public defenders - United States 2. Justice - United
    States 3. Poor - United States
    I. Title
    364' .086942'0973

Library of Congress Cataloging-in-Publication Data
Emmelman, Debra S., 1952-
    Justice for the poor : a study of criminal defense work / Debra S. Emmelman.
        p. cm. -- (Law, justice, and power)
    Includes bibliographical references and index.
    ISBN 0-7546-2309-2 (alk. paper)
        1. Public defenders--United States. 2. Legal assistance to the poor--United States. 3.
    Plea bargaining--United States. 4. Criminal justice, Administration of--United States. I.
    Title. II. Series.

    KF9646 .E47 2003
    345.73'01--dc

                                                                                    2002034534

ISBN 0 7546 2309 2

Printed and bound in Great Britain by Biddles Ltd, *www.biddles.co.uk*

Contents

Acknowledgements

This book would never have been completed without the aid and support of a large number of people. I can only hope to mention here a few who have been especially helpful.

I would like to begin by thanking Joseph R. Gusfield, to whom I have always looked for intellectual inspiration, wisdom and guidance. He has never failed me in any of these respects but instead has always exceeded my expectations. His fair and patient manners are also characteristics that I both deeply admire in any human being and am extremely grateful to find in a person of such high stature. He is a mentor in the truest sense.

I would also like to thank Jacqueline Wiseman whose conscientious appraisal of my work resulted in a number of both helpful criticisms as well as greatly appreciated praises. Her supportive yet tactfully critical stance has not merely enabled me to produce a much more articulate and carefully developed analysis, but also brought me out of some of my bleakest moments. She has been a trusted and respected confidante as well as a superb role model.

I also owe a great deal to the Defenders, whose actual names I am not at liberty to mention here. These attorneys were enormously helpful and remarkably accommodating, especially as they sought to teach me about their profession through the long and tedious interviewing process. They also reaffirmed my faith in, and hope for, humankind by showing me that sometimes the poor really have talented and devoted champions.

I am also grateful to previous publishers of copyrighted work for permission to reproduce material here as well as the editors and reviewers of journals in which articles appeared. I cannot say how much the exacting standards and patience of the latter persons contributed to my growth as a researcher and scholar. Among the material that derived and benefited from these enterprises are most of Chapter Five (originally appearing in Volume 30, Number 2 of *Law and Society Review* and reprinted here with the permission of the Law and Society Association); most of Chapter Three (originally appearing in Volume 22, Number 4 of *Law and Social Inquiry*, published by the University of Chicago Press, © 1997 by the American Bar Foundation, all rights reserved); and portions of Chapters One, Two and Six which originally appeared in Volume 18, Number 2 of the *Criminal Justice Review* (published by The College of Public and Urban Affairs at Georgia State University and reprinted here with permission), Volume 17, Number 1 of *Symbolic Interaction* (© 1994 by JAI Press, Inc, and reprinted here with permission from the University of California Press), and the anthology *For the Common Good: A Critical Examination of Law and Social Control* (edited by R. Robin Miller and Sandra Lee Browning, published by Carolina Academic Press, 2003 and reprinted here with permission).

Others have made important contributions as well. Michael Butler, John Critzer and Shirley Varmette have all provided some very useful editorial comments and much appreciated moral support. Kirsten Weissenberg and Pam Bertram of Ashgate Publishing provided invaluable advice concerning the production of camera-ready copy. I am also indebted to Stuart Hadden, William Burgan, Daryl Osborne, Wendy Rappaport, Terry Osborn, D.J. Watson, Christopher Doob, Thomas Weinberg as well as members of my family for simply 'being there' and believing in me.

I would also like to express gratitude to Southern Connecticut State University for awarding me a sabbatical during which I completed this manuscript and to Austin Sarat who read and then proposed the manuscript to Ashgate Publishing Ltd. for publication in the *Law, Justice and Power* series.

Last but far from least, I want to extend my utmost gratitude to my husband, Theodore T. Smith. His countless readings and seemingly endless editing of this manuscript, his patience and consideration as I spent interminable hours sitting in front of my computer, and his unfailing encouragement throughout the process of producing this book have never ceased to amaze me. I am very lucky to have him in my life.

I could not have produced this book without the aid and support of all the people mentioned here. At the same time, I cannot say that I followed everyone's advice completely or flawlessly. Consequently, any errors in this book should be seen as the author's sole responsibility.

Foreword

In 1963 the United States Supreme Court reversed an earlier decision and extended the right to legal assistance from defendants in capital cases to those in felony cases as well. It was initiated by the actions of a prisoner, Clarence Gideon, and argued by the Supreme Court-appointed attorney, Abe Fortas (later a Supreme Court justice himself). The decision marked a distinct progression toward efforts to eliminate the disadvantages of indigent defendants in obtaining the justice that a fair trial would ensure. It guaranteed that everywhere in the United States poverty was not a barrier to adequate legal counsel.

Clarence Gideon was a poor man of limited education. He had a record of past convictions and prison for felonies. At his original trial, he had maintained to the judge that his was not a fair trial because he could not afford a lawyer and none had been provided for him. Acting as his own lawyer, he claimed that his constitutional right had been denied. In his petition to the Supreme Court he stated the issue to which Debra Emmelman's absorbing study is devoted:

> It makes no difference how old I am or what color I am or what church I belong to if any. The question is I did not get a fair trial. (Anthony Lewis, Gideon's Trumpet, 1964, pp. 37–38)

What is a 'fair trial'? Does adequate counsel assure fairness? Debra Emmelman's study of defense attorneys operating under contract with local courts reminds us of the complexities of 'fairness'. 'Law on the books' requires a level plane in which the prosecution and the defense appear as adversaries and the prosecution is governed as much by a sense of achieving justice as by winning cases. In this form the structure is 'loaded' in the direction of the defendant. Innocence need not be proved but guilt must be established 'beyond a reasonable doubt'. The onus is on the prosecution.

A more realistic view has been at variance with this view. It suggests that prosecutors and defense attorneys are more interested in winning than in achieving a just decision. Past studies have suggested that defense attorneys are bound to cooperate with prosecution in clearing dockets; that they are co-opted into being helpful rather than adversarial. Equal treatment before the law is foiled by the organizational structure of the courts, the prosecution and the defense bar.

It is also the case that criticism has been directed at the processes of plea bargaining and settlements under which the right to trial is bypassed by negotiations between prosecution and defense. Under such bargaining the defendant pleads guilty to a charge and both defense and prosecution avoid trial. The defendant ostensibly gains a lighter sentence than a trial is likely to offer. Thus the right to a trial is meaningless. The 'real' disposition goes on in the settlement process.

It has long been recognized that most criminal as well as civil cases are decided by settlements between adversaries. Trials are rare events. In criminal cases plea bargaining and the determination of charges is the most common result. Emmelman, as is true of several past studies, also finds the importance of negotiated settlements. Like other studies, she does not thereby negate the importance of the trial. The trial is crucial to the bargaining process itself. How the defendant is seen as likely to fare before a jury has much to do with what the defense attorneys studied here call 'the value of a case' – the kind of settlement that is attainable.

It is here, in the bargaining process, that the relation between prosecution and defense becomes important to the fairness of the process. If the defense attorney is obligated to the prosecution or the court then his/her adversarial function is colored in the direction of prosecutorial wishes. This was the conclusion in Abraham Blumberg's classic study of defense lawyers (1967) as practicing a 'confidence game' in which they were 'double agents' convincing the defendant into accepting pleas. In this defense attorneys helped the prosecution to gain resolution of cases without the costs of time and money entailed by a trial. Emmelman's study finds this is not the case in the agency she studied in the late 1980s.

In her observations, defense attorneys and prosecutors were involved in a process of opposition clearly in keeping with the legal commitment to adversarial relations. Each tried to do the best they could; the defense attorney attempted to gain the best result s/he could for his/her client; the prosecutor to exact the toughest result s/he could. They were both affected by the value of the case – by what in their judgment was a better outcome than a trial might bring or when a trial was warranted. Ultimately the client or the prosecutor's supervisor had the final word and the lawyer the obligation to advise his/her client. The usefulness of the lawyer to the defendant and his/her support of indigent defendants are in keeping with the concept of a 'fair trial' and might even have pleased Clarence Gideon.

The problem of obtaining 'fairness,' as Emmelman realizes, go well beyond the issue of lawyers and adversarialness. The observation of this is of great value and is the chief contribution of this book to the ongoing discussion of how to gain a justice system that is as fair to the poor as it is to the rich. Aspects of class division in American society loom large and affect the operations of the criminal justice system in ways that stem from American social structure and are difficult to eradicate short of changing that structure itself.

The rich detail and the accounts of specific cases in Professor Emmelman's study enables us to see how the diversities of class affect the process of bargaining by creating a sense of what a trial is likely to yield. The people the defense bar speaks for are not the same as those who will constitute their juries in the event of a trial. Not only are the defendants poor; they are less educated, less aware of the court and legal procedure, of the manners and language that are the staples of a more stable and employed citizenry. What's more the defendants are also more likely to have a criminal record. In addition, the interpretation of behavior given by such diversities makes for sharp differences between the jury or the judge and the defendant. What is conventional for the defendant may well be perceived differently by juries and judges. These unavoidable qualities color the jury's perception of the actions to which the defendant is charged. In the very term 'prejudicial' they are pre-judgments.

I was struck some years ago in observing an arraignment court of the sharp differences in class that clothing represents. Doing research on the sentencing of drinking-driving offenders, I observed courtrooms in San Diego. Walking into the courtroom it was quite easy to know who were the lawyers and who were the defendants, especially for the men. Male lawyers wore jackets, dress shirts and ties. Male defendants hardly ever wore jackets or ties and often only a sport shirt and nondescript trousers. Either defendants owned only the most casual of clothing or were unaware of the manners and dress expectations of a courtroom. (It is notable that drinking-driving offenders are a higher income group than the modal or average criminal.)

Emmelman raises these issues of fairness in her conclusion. They are embedded in the very nature of what social structure means. Perhaps greater attention to obtaining more representative juries might be one means of gaining more of the fairness that Gideon sought. It is the virtue of this study that it has put the spotlight of research on to the problem and raised the issue to realistic inquiry.

Joseph Gusfield
La Jolla, California

Chapter One

Introduction

An important issue in law and society is whether or not our legal system accords justice to poor criminal defendants.[1] Much of the research on this matter focuses on the conduct of publicly provided defense attorneys and reaffirms popular stereotypes of them. The classic studies of Sudnow (1965) and Blumberg (1967a; 1967b), for example, assert that because their careers hinge largely on cooperative relationships with others members of the court system, lawyers for the poor sacrifice adversarial ideals and induce their clients to plead guilty. Others have found that such factors as high case loads and inadequate funding,[2] the attorney's desire to maximize her income,[3] political co-option[4] and the failure to secure pretrial release[5] undermine the ethical representation of indigent persons.

Despite all the discrediting attestations, the preponderance of research on attorneys' behavior appears to indicate that, in general, publicly provided lawyers are equally as, if not more effective than, other lawyers. For example, many have found that decisions to plea bargain are *not* perfunctory but instead based on legally appropriate considerations.[6] Similarly, others conclude that attorneys for the poor achieve the same, and sometimes better results than private attorneys,[7] and a few analysts have gone so far as to argue that aspects of indigent defense systems actually encourage adversarialness and ethical relationships with clients.[8]

Nevertheless, both casual and formal observations reveal that the poor are more likely to be convicted of crime and to receive more severe sanctions than other types of defendants.[9] Assuming that their attorneys behave responsibly, the question that arises is why the poor are more likely to receive these censures. Should we conclude that they are more likely to *commit* crime and therefore they are simply receiving their 'just desserts'? Or might we conclude that something else is unduly tipping the scales of justice against them?

Examining these latter possibilities, investigators employing positivist methodologies have considered whether and how social class as an *extra-legal variable* influences adjudicative results. Among these studies, some have found that a defendant's socioeconomic status has little or no relationship to criminal case outcomes,[10] while others conclude that class has at least *some* important influence.[11]

Adopting a more critical approach to this concern, Neo-Marxist scholars have considered how *the legal system itself* is used to disguise and perpetuate class injustice. For example, Chambliss' (1964) investigation of the changes in the vagrancy statute during the fourteenth and sixteenth centuries and E.P. Thompson's (1975) analysis of the Black Act during the eighteenth century both show how the early English legal system was used to promote the interests of the dominant class at the expense of the less powerful. Similarly, Hay's (1975) study of eighteenth century English court rituals reveals how that legal system was used to bring about the illusion of justice in order to maintain oppressive class relations.[12]

This book is a study of justice for the poor. Focusing on the behavior of one group of court-appointed defense attorneys (hereafter referred to as 'Defenders'), it considers how indigent defendants' social class influences criminal case outcomes. It does this by examining both the place of law and the place of social class in the lawyers' everyday negotiation of criminal cases. In the end, this book assesses not merely whether social class *undermines* justice ideals but moreover whether the socio-legal environment itself somehow *obfuscates and reinforces* class oppression.

An Everyday Life Approach to Justice for the Poor

I examine attorneys' behavior here from the standpoint of 'law in everyday life.' As Sarat and Kearns explain, when we examine law in everyday life

> we speak about routine, habit, convention, and the constraints
> and restraints that each imposes. We confront law in its
> dailiness and as a virtually invisible factor in social life
> (1995b: 1).

From this viewpoint, law is neither external to nor wholly constitutive of the everyday world. Instead, it is produced and reproduced in day-to-day encounters and becomes part of the everyday world to the extent that it enters social actors' consciousness and they make it so. Yet permeating daily routines, it also becomes part of the taken-for-granted and therefore not-altogether-obvious social environment.[13]

While law from the perspective of everyday life entails some degree of social consensus (otherwise, how could legal actors interact and agree upon anything?), it is also a *negotiated* reality. Gusfield perhaps best describes this in his discussion of the crime of drinking and driving:

The idea of law as a statement of a moral reality, a consensus about acceptable and unacceptable behavior, is seemingly contradicted in the process by which the drinking-driving event becomes a 'fact' in judicial practice. Here it is a negotiated reality, not a clear and consistently discovered event. It is a result of values, organizational constraints, pragmatic contingencies, and bargaining between the relevant parties, considerations that make it a matter of the choice, discretion, and power of the several parties interacting in the process of law. It is in this sense that 'driving while under the influence of alcohol' is a social construction – a creation of human beings and not a direct representation of an objective fact (1981:133).

Given an everyday life approach to law, how are we to determine whether Defenders behave ethically? Clearly, it would be tautological to assess this matter on the basis of whether they practice law in a manner consistent with the way they understand it. Consequently, what is instead contemplated is simply what role law and adversarial procedures, *in fact,* play throughout their daily routines: by examining their everyday conduct, we will ascertain the extent to which law and legal procedures enter into the attorneys' consciousness and how these legal considerations influence their relationships with clients and their advocacy behavior in general.

Similarly, how are we to determine whether poor defendants' social class influences adjudicative outcomes in some other manner? From the perspective of everyday life, social class does not exist apart from actors' interpretations of situations but instead is part and parcel of them: it is an ongoing, lived and socially managed experience. Like law and everyday life, these experiences permeate the criminal court system and, if social class affects legal cases, it must be seen to do so somehow through court actors' sensibilities and performances. Thus, in this study, we will consider not simply *whether* social class influences adjudicative outcomes but, if it does, *how* it enters into the attorneys' consciousness and influences their advocacy behavior.

The Place of Culture in the Analysis of Justice for the Poor

In recent years, social scientists have experienced a number of problems in their attempt to define culture and its relationship with law.[14] All the same, as Sarat and Kearns (1998b) point out, the central focus in contemporary times appears to be on 'meaning' which not only organizes human social interaction[15] but also is nested within some type of larger, more encompassing symbolic frame of reference. As explained by Clifford Geertz,

> Our gaze focuses on meaning, on the ways ... (people) make sense of what they do – practically, morally, expressively, ... juridically – by setting it within larger frames of signification, and how they keep those larger frames in place or try to, by organizing what they do in terms of them (quoted in Sarat and Kearns, 1998b: 6).

Despite the fact that culture entails some type of shared symbolic system or frame of signification, it is also understood in contemporary times that no such system is universal or shared equally among all members of a society.[16] Thus, no single culture constitutes the *only* possible set of ideas and symbols with which human groups may understand their experiences. Even so, culture *does* place constraints on the number of available interpretations that actors may employ. As explained by Silbey,

> [A] person may express, through words or actions, a multifaceted, contradictory and variable legal consciousness ... [However,] ... The possible variations in consciousness are limited, that is, situationally and organizationally circumscribed. Rather than talking about meaning making as an individualized process, cultural analysis emphasizes the limited number of available interpretations for assigning meaning to things and events within any situation or setting. Similarly, access to and experience within the situations from which interpretations emerge are differentially available. Here attention to consciousness emphasizes its collective construction and the constraints operating in any particular setting or community as well as the subject's work in making interpretations and affixing meanings (1992: 44–45).

Overall then, culture can be seen as a type of structured symbolic system that social actors employ to understand, navigate and communicate in their social worlds. As such, it can also be seen as a type of signification or *language* system.

Perhaps the best and most useful depiction of culture as a type of language system is provided in the work of Kenneth Burke,[17] who argues that social action is predicated in language systems. These language systems are types of linguistic frameworks and enterprises which are identifiable by clusters of terms and which involve speech in its various forms. However, these systems also include nonlinguistic symbols. Thus, Burke's concept of 'language system' appears to refer more generally to symbolic systems or cultural domains of meaning.

Furthermore, Burke argues that social actors are engaged in 'rhetoric' or strategies of persuasion that are grounded in language systems. As explained by Gusfield,

> Burke's importance for the sociologist is especially important in his conception of human action as rhetorical...We cannot avoid rhetoric. When we speak, act, dress, eat and generally conduct our lives we communicate and, in doing so, persuade others, including ourselves. Seen, in Burke's frequently used phrase, 'as strategies for situations' human events involve an actor and an audience. Action is seen as persuasional and therefore rhetorical (1989:17).

Unlike Goffman's dramaturgy,[18] Burke's dramatism places more emphasis on language and on the use of language in interaction. Additionally, social actors appear to exercise relatively less discretion or intention in Burke's view of social life insofar as they are somewhat blind to and imprisoned in the cultural frameworks or language systems they employ. This constraint is what Burke refers to as the 'grammar' of social action, a type of syntax that sets limits on social actors' understanding of situations as well as their ability to communicate and take certain actions. Unlike Goffman's dramaturgy, an awareness of these constraints is prescribed in Burke's dramatism and thus makes their critique possible. Moreover, for Burke, the cultural domains or language systems within which social actors behave imply valuations and accordingly, social and moral hierarchies. Hence, Burke's conceptualization of social action appears to entail greater overall coupling with broader social and political conditions than Goffman's.

In this study, the cultural analysis of justice for the poor entails an examination of not simply meaning but of *cultural domains of meaning* that are shared to a greater or lesser extent among various social groups. These domains enable Defenders not merely to interpret phenomena in their everyday legal practices but moreover to help create, maintain and perpetuate the reality of the legal system in general and the criminal court system in particular. Yet while these domains of meaning permit Defenders to construct a legal reality, they also constrain their behavior and the type of world they are able to bring about. In particular, Defenders are obligated to employ cultural rhetoric which consists of the terminologies and taxonomies of the status quo and which compels a definition of reality consistent with the prevailing social order. As a consequence, the narratives or stories they provide on behalf of their clients inadequately describe and reflect the situations of poor criminal suspects. As Amsterdam and Bruner state,

> A lawyer's work is full of narrative labor designed to cook up 'winning' stories according to hornbook recipes ... An inevitable consequence of such adversarial storytelling is that it tends to focus the attention of storytellers and hearers alike upon certain considerations rather than others, and to put a premium on type-casting the elements of every tale to fit the stock model of the 'relevant' considerations (2000:118).

Thus, we will find in this study that despite Defenders' efforts to protect and assert their clients' rights, the voices of the poor are frequently muted, precluded and/or shrouded in insinuations of culpability throughout everyday legal routines while the voice of the status quo takes precedence.[19] This situation as well as the place of cultural analysis in this study is summarized nicely in the words of Sarat and Kearns:

> If we think of legal argument as providing an opportunity for the display of character and the constitution of community, it is also important to recognize that, in the space of law, not all characters or voices are welcome and among those that are welcome not all are equally valued...This quality of rhetoric opens the way for an inquiry into new questions of justice and for an effort to link the rhetoric of law to its operation as a system of power in which power is defined in terms of what can be spoken and what is silenced. Here we are invited to recognize the fact that law is both a privileged discourse and a discourse of the privileged (1996:12–13).

This book examines the role of culture in legal negotiations of justice for poor criminal suspects. In so doing, it is an attempt to restore the voices of the powerless and establish justice on their behalf.

Research Methods

The data for this study were originally collected between September of 1984 and September of 1988 in a criminal court jurisdiction located in a large urban area on the west coast. (This area will be referred to as 'Smith City'.) At the time of the study, the system for defending indigent persons in Smith City consisted of a limited Public Defender's Office, a Central Office of Defense Services, and a private contract system. The corporation studied (referred to as 'Defense Alliance') was one of the many private contract groups in the area. It differed from the others, however, in three important ways: first, it was the largest contract group; it had four different offices which covered three different jurisdictions, and it employed approximately 36 attorneys overall at any one time. Second, unlike the other contract groups, it was a *non-profit* corporation. Finally, this corporation had a reputation in the criminal justice community for providing high quality defense service to indigent persons.[20]

The population studied consisted of all the attorneys employed at the downtown branch of this corporation. Approximately 15 attorneys were employed at any given time in that office. Approximately half of the attorneys were women. Their ages ranged from early thirties to the early fifties, with the average age in the late thirties. With the exception of one African-American attorney, who worked at this office for only a brief time, all of the attorneys were white. All but one of the attorneys handled felony cases.

Entry into the setting was gained through an internship program carried out between the university and the defense corporation. (The author was a graduate student at the time.) Having acquired permission to conduct research both formally (from the University's Human Subjects Committee) as well as informally (from the attorneys who participated in the study), data were initially collected through participant observation: for an average of about eight hours per week, I observed the Defenders' behavior while serving as a student intern and law clerk.

As a student intern and law clerk, I was permitted to observe virtually every aspect of the Defenders' behavior – including that which occurred in such behind-the-scenes places as the attorneys' offices, judges' chambers and jail. These attorneys also accepted me as an 'insider' to the extent that some extended invitations to attend parties or other get-togethers. Only one attorney appeared to regard me with any suspicion.

Throughout the observation period, field notes were recorded and then later analyzed through a grounded theory methodology. Specifically, field notes were coded and then examined for underlying patterns. Each pattern was then described in a memo, and all the memos were then compared and contrasted to ascertain more fundamental as well as co-occurring behavior patterns.[21] In order to clarify and refine these preliminary research findings, in-depth interviews were then conducted toward the end of the study.

The interviews were designed to ascertain the manner in which the Defenders routinely defend criminal cases. To avoid predisposing their responses and thereby biasing the findings, questions were open-ended and phrased as neutrally as possible. After some preliminary questions regarding their background and general perceptions of other court actors, for example, the interview began with the question 'What do you typically do with a case once you have received it? How do you typically handle it?'

All the attorneys who were currently employed by the corporation (five men and six women) as well as four ex-Defenders (three men and one woman) participated in the interviews. The interviews lasted between three and a half and four hours. All the interviews were taped, transcribed and then later analyzed.

It is important to emphasize here the value of the interviews to this study. Much of the behavior under scrutiny was tacit and taken-for-granted by the attorneys, and the researcher did not have a legal background with which to fathom its existence. In addition, the attorneys talked about certain issues only when wondering aloud about certain matters in a case or when explaining to clients why a particular course of action was desirable. Consequently, many insights emerged in rather cryptic bits and pieces throughout the observational analysis and a thorough and complete understanding required careful probing and elaboration during interviews.

Clearly, a major weakness in this study is that the research population is not representative of either all criminal defense attorneys or even all criminal defense attorneys who represent indigent persons. However, an important strength of the study is that it sheds new light on largely elusive behaviors that may very well be prevalent among a substantial number of other defense attorneys. It is hoped that this study will encourage further research on larger, more representative samples of attorneys.

Organization of the Book

The findings of this study are reviewed in five chapters. In Chapter Two, I examine how Defenders anticipate or look upon their task. Specifically, I describe how they view their cultural arena, which includes their own as well as others' roles, the obstacles they perceive themselves to confront, and the cultural 'tools' or language systems that they anticipate they must employ.

Given the broader cultural context for behavior, Chapter Three describes how Defenders develop professional opinions of specific cases and decide whether any single case should be plea bargained or taken to trial. Herein, we see how certain cultural considerations and concerns are enacted mentally prior to taking some type of action.

Chapter Four and Chapter Five discuss how the cultural battles among the legal professionals take place. In Chapter Four, I discuss how Defenders take cases to trial. I examine how the Defenders negotiate plea bargains in Chapter Five. At issue throughout these chapters are not only whether poor defendants appear to encounter any injustice but also whether one mode of case disposition appears to result in any greater injustice than the other.

In Chapter Six, I provide an overview of the findings and discuss them in terms of their implications for future research and social reform.

Notes

1   For a good discussion on the place of justice in law and legal theory, see Sarat and Kearns (1998a).
2   E.g., Guggenheim (1986), Lerner (1986) and Nelson (1988).
3   E.g., Alschuler (1975; 1986) and Blumberg (1967b).
4   E.g., Platt and Pollock (1974).
5   E.g., Swigert and Farrell (1977) and Holmes, Daudistel and Farrell (1987).
6   E.g., Heumann (1975), Mather (1979), McDonald (1985), Neubauer (1974), and Rosett and Cressey (1976).
7   E.g., Feeley (1979), Hermann et al (1977), Wheeler and Wheeler (1980) and Wice (1985).
8   See Emmelman (1993), Flemming (1986), McIntyre (1987) and Skolnick (1967).
9   See, for example, Beirne and Messerschmidt (1995) and Reiman (1998).
10 E.g., Bernstein et al (1977), Chiricos and Waldo (1975), Eisenstein and Jacob (1977), Hagan (1974), Holmes et al (1987), Myers (1980) and Willick et al (1975).
11 E.g., Clarke and Koch (1976), Cooney (1994), Farrell (1971), Hagan (1974), Jankovic (1978), Kalven and Zeisel (1976), Kruttschnitt (1980), Lizotte (1978), Reskin and Visher (1986), and Swigert and Farrell (1977).
12 For other examples of research in this tradition, see Balbus, (1973), Beirne and Quinney (1982), Hall (1952), Hay et al (1975), Jeffery (1957) and Reiman (1998).
13 For more discussion on this matter, see Ewick and Silbey (1998), Sarat and Kearns (1995b), and Silbey (1985).
14 For discussions on this issue, see Coombe (1998), Harris (1999), Hays (2000), Sarat and Kearns (1998b and 1998c) and Swingewood (1998).
15 For additional discussion on how social actors make meaning and thereby organize their

behavior and society in general, see Berger and Luckmann (1967), Blumer (1978), Garfinkle (1967), Mehan and Wood (1975), and Schutz (1962).

16 For more discussion on this issue, see Coombe (1998).

17 See Burke (1969; 1989), Carrier (1982), Gusfield (1989), Littlejohn (1977) and Overington (1977) for more details on Burke's dramatism.

18 See, for example, Goffman (1959; 1963).

19 For overviews and examples of works on legal narrative and the rhetoric of law, see Amsterdam and Bruner (2000), Sarat and Kearns (1996) and Ewick and Silbey (1995).

20 For further discussion on this issue, see Emmelman (1993) as well as the conclusion to this book.

21 See Glaser and Strauss (1967) and Lester and Hadden (1980) for further details on the use of this methodology.

Chapter Two

Anticipating the Task:
The Cultural Context for Behavior

The Defender's world consists of people who come together to create the reality of the criminal court. This reality is created through cultural systems of meaning that are shared among all court actors to varying extents. Employing these cultural systems, Defenders interpret their own and others' roles. This understanding then makes up their sense of the task-at-hand and comprises the cultural context for their negotiations.

There are six types of court actors who appear in the Defenders' consciousness as most influential in adjudication proceedings. These are the Defenders themselves, the Assistant or Deputy District Attorneys (hereafter referred to as D.A.s or prosecutors), judges, the jury, indigent defendants, and witnesses. For each of these actors, three kinds of behavior emerge as characteristic: role prerequisite behavior, macro-referenced behavior and cultural fluency.

Role Prerequisite Behaviors

Role prerequisite behaviors are taken-for-granted understandings about 'who' the key players are in the court system and (in general) what they do. These beliefs make the reality of the criminal court system possible: like incorrigible propositions,[1] they not only define the roles of court actors in the first place but also facilitate the symbolic interaction that creates the social world of the court.

The Defender's Role Prerequisite Behavior

The fundamental grounds not only for court-appointed but for all types of defense attorneys *is* defense. Therefore, it should be no surprise that the most important prerequisite behavior which the Defenders perceive of themselves is advocacy on behalf of accused persons: everything that these attorneys do in their capacity as defense attorneys is logically and professionally related to the principle of defense. This does not mean, however, that complete vindication for their clients is always the goal. Instead, it simply means that everything they do can somehow be regarded as 'championing the cause' of criminal suspects – even if it only entails attempting to reduce slightly through plea-bargaining the costs that a defendant would be liable to incur otherwise.

Two other behaviors that are also basic to their role are counseling and mediation.[2] First, because they are specialists who possess expertise regarding a legal system that is somewhat opaque to and exacting of their clients, Defenders are compelled to advise clients not only about their legal rights and responsibilities, but also about the 'soundness' of their case and the best defense strategy.[3] Second, in their attempts to assert as well as protect their clients' interests, they translate communications originating from the defendant to other key participants in the court system as well as translate communications issued from other participants in the court system to the defendant. Thus, as Sarat and Felstiner (1986) found regarding divorce lawyers, the Defenders act as types of *cultural translators* for their clients.

The Defenders' role prerequisite behaviors were described by two of these attorneys in the following comments:[4]

> Ingmar: It doesn't make any difference that [I am] court-appointed. As a defense attorney, my job is to be an advocate for my client. And as I tell them when I first get their case ... I am to advise them, make sure they understand all the options, what is happening to them, what their rights are, what could happen to them, what choices they have, and I'm also advising them as to what I think the best thing for them to do is and why. And I run the case. I decide what the defense is going to be, and how it's going to be presented, and what witnesses are going to be presented.

> LuAnn: I tell my clients–my job is to see that they get hurt as little as possible. Which means that even if they're not guilty, probably no one is going to send them a bouquet of flowers and an apology ... I explain to them what's going on and what I think their chances are. If they're gonna do something stupid, they'll know they're doing it and not me.

The D.A.'s Role Prerequisite Behavior

Research indicates that the D.A. has the most powerful role in the court system:[5] it is the D.A. who decides whether charges will be brought against the defendant in the first place and whether a case will be prosecuted to the fullest. Accordingly, if there were no D.A. (or anyone like him or her), there would be nobody to press criminal charges, no need for criminal defense attorneys, and certainly our court system, as we know it would cease to exist.

Ironically, while we can see that the D.A.'s role in our adversarial system of justice is to prosecute defendants, Defenders envision the D.A.'s ideal role in terms allied more closely with their own. Specifically, they maintain that the D.A. is *supposed* to cooperate with the defense in an effort to seek truth and justice. Nevertheless, they all agree that the D.A.'s *actual* role is to prosecute or somehow aggravate the case against the defendant.[6] This is illustrated in two Defenders' comments:

> William: I would *like* to think that the D.A.'s role should be to seek justice and to protect the citizen from criminal types, and things of that nature. Practically speaking ... it seems as if their role is ... a very narrow, almost automaton type of role where all they have in their minds is prosecute and convict, prosecute and convict. It shouldn't be that way.

> Vera: The role of the D.A. is, the way I see the role is, the D.A.'s there to give me a hard time. The D.A. is there ... to exaggerate the facts, to exaggerate the seriousness of the situation.

The Judge's Role Prerequisite Behavior

As may be obvious (and yet probably taken-for-granted), the judge's role prerequisite behavior is that of 'pronouncing judgment', or, deciding on issues which emerge between the defense attorney and the D.A. As Ingmar explained,

> They totally decide whatever issues in front of them – whether it's a motion, or about bail, or about whether there's an illegal search and seizure, or whether the person should go to prison, or if you have a court trial [on] that issue, or an evidentiary issue, whatever. They clearly make those

decisions. [Interviewer: Jury trial?] They make rulings on all
the evidentiary issues.

As Ingmar's comments suggest, judges decide two types of issues with
regard to the adjudication of guilt. These are issues of law and issues of fact.
Issues of law concern disputes such as those over search and seizure and
whether the defendant should be bound over for trial. In debates concerning
fact, the judge weighs the evidence put forth by the attorneys and decides
which one has proven his or her case.[7]

Although all judges perform the same role prerequisite behavior, they do not
do so in precisely the same ways. Thus, in an apparent effort to reduce the
uncertainty surrounding their behavior, Defenders particularize their
perceptions by focusing on important adjudication patterns that distinguish
among judges. They make two types of distinctions: those regarding a judge's
competence in conducting specific types of proceedings (e.g., good trial
judges) and those regarding judges' biases toward certain types of crimes
(e.g., judges who are on a crusade against child abuse and therefore deal more
harshly with those cases). This is illustrated in the following comments:

> Janet: I have this guy [i.e., case] right now ... In this case, I
> pled the guy, he had these awful problems that really made
> it, it could not have gotten any better, and *I figured this judge
> would have been a good sentencing judge*, and I'll just get
> together a good sentencing package ... and get all that
> information in front of the judge. [Emphasis added.]

> William: [Interviewer: Different judges are better or worse?]
> That's correct. There are better settlement judges *as it relates
> to different kinds of cases*. Some judges have seen so much
> – say a child molest case – have seen so many of them, that
> if you have one that just involves digital manipulation as
> opposed to rape or sodomy, and your client has no record ...
> [they are much more reasonable than others] [Emphasis
> added.]

As these comments suggest, Defenders behold judges as types of *reference
persons* for their own decision making: in deciding on the best defense tactic
for their clients, Defenders draw upon their understanding of what a judge will
probably do.[8]

The Jury's Role Prerequisite Behavior

The jury in a criminal case is expected to act as the judge of evidence brought forth during a trial. (There are no judge trials in Smith City.) For cases in which the Defenders are involved, the jury consists of twelve people selected from the community to carry-out this task in a collective manner. The jury's role differs from judges' because jurors are not accorded the right or responsibility to 'decide the law'; the jury does not decide what laws are at issue in a case, whether a particular law is valid, or how the law should be applied. Nevertheless, because their clients might invoke their constitutional right to a jury trial any time prior to a formal finding of guilt, and because the jury might be employed to ward off the threat of capricious and oppressive decision-making on the part of judges and prosecutors, Defenders regard the jury's role *very* seriously. In fact, the jury's role is not limited solely to those rather infrequent times when a case goes to trial but instead is prominent throughout much of the Defenders' routines.

In his study of the criminal court system in Prairie City, David Neubauer (1974) found that defense and prosecuting attorneys shape the procedural rights available to defendants through their use of three mutually shared standards for negotiation. Among these are 'standards of proof assumed to be maintained by juries'. Defenders employ the same standard: because the jury plays such an important role in the adjudication of guilt, they postulate the jury's point of view toward the evidence in cases *regardless* of whether a case actually goes to trial. Thus, similar to judges, the jury exists in the Defender's mind as a kind of *reference group* for evaluating evidence.[9] Two Defenders explained this in the following manner:

> Ingmar: [Juries are] the ultimate judges of fact in a trial – not of the law. They're supposed to apply the law that the judge gives to them to the facts that they decide. So they are the ultimate judge of the facts and whatever ruling they make on the facts never changes through appeal or what have you ... you know in all cases that out there you could have a jury. Their existence is always postulated in every case. You can tell your client, 'Look. Do you think this is gonna sell to a jury?'

> LuAnn: I think that the first thing you assess in a case is whether it will fly in front of a jury. Because, you have to decide whether a case is triable or not. Because if it's not

triable, then that's gonna affect your strategy through the whole handling of it.

The Witness's Role Prerequisite Behavior

The most critical role prerequisite behavior for witnesses is that of providing evidence: any witness in a criminal case testifies or 'bears witness' to a matter which could suggest either a defendant's innocence or guilt. As Nora and Kathy explained,

> Kathy: The witness is essential. The state of the witnesses in a way are the state of the case because witnesses are the way that evidence comes into a trial and that witness shapes the evidence.

> Nora: Usually [the witness's role is] just to report what they saw. If they're a complaining witness, they may be complaining about some wrong that's been done.

As Kathy indicates, the important role of witnesses in criminal cases cannot be over-emphasized. Not only is their testimony considered evidence, but they also introduce and define all other non-human evidentiary components. In essence, there *is* no evidence without witnesses. And without evidence, of course, there is no criminal case.

The Indigent Defendant's Role Prerequisite Behavior

The Defenders view their clients as accused persons who require professional legal counsel and advocacy. If they did not view them in this manner, obviously their services would not be required and their occupational reality would dissolve. Nevertheless, these lawyers also expect their clients to assist them with, or more precisely, to provide significant input regarding their defenses. In essence, the two actors are expected to work together throughout the entire adjudication process. This is illustrated in the following comments:

> Ingmar: [Interviewer: Other than telling you what he wants, what other role does the defendant play?] Well, he's got to tell me what he knows about the case. And ... from everything he says, I make sure that I discuss with him what I see the defense is and what he thinks about it and what

witnesses may be available ... and we also talk about things in terms of his life ... Because I can't advise him ... without knowing something about him. So, I mean I have to have all that input from him ... And then there's other things that come up. Medical problems. Drugs. Do they have psychiatric or psychological problems? I need to find out about that ... and have psychologists or psychiatrists appointed so they can evaluate him and get me a confidential report back which may be useful in sentencing, or possibly for the trial itself.

Steve: I always ask [the defendant] for his version [of the incident]. [Interviewer: Does his version structure the defense?] A good percentage of the time. Sometimes we have to ignore their viewpoint because it doesn't fall within a legally recognized defense. That's again why the defendant shouldn't be his own attorney.

Although the Defenders are court-appointed and therefore advocate on behalf of indigent persons, the characteristic of 'indigence' does not itself appear to imply any role prerequisite behavior. Nevertheless, indigence *does* play an important role throughout much of their everyday routines. The details of this will be provided subsequently in this chapter.

In 1967, Skolnick argued that the adversarial system of justice rests on the assumption of conflict and that the norm of conflict has been institutionalized in the courts. This study finds that the norm of conflict is institutionalized to at least some extent through court actors' role-prerequisite behaviors: It is the Defender's role *as* a defense attorney to advocate for as well as counsel and mediate on behalf of a person accused of wrongdoing. This role, of course, presupposes a defendant as well as some type of prosecutor – a role assumed by the District Attorney. Moreover, both the judge and the jury's roles presuppose the presence of some type of 'combatants' upon whose behaviors they must make a judgment. Finally, apart from witnesses who provide evidence regarding matters, there is no matter to contest in the first place. Thus, the role prerequisite behaviors described above are cultural understandings, which are essential not only for symbolic interaction among these actors but moreover for the operation of our adversarial system of justice as we understand it today.

Macro-Referenced Behavior

Macro-referenced behavior is conduct that Defenders perceive to stem from social practices or conditions located somewhere outside of the immediate court milieu. It corresponds to one type of 'macro reference' elaborated upon by Randall Collins. Specifically, it is what Collins calls a 'situational macro view' (1981:97), whereby people in small-scale interpretive situations take account of the macro social structure either by referring to other small-scale situations or to more reified macro-concepts such as 'the economy' or 'the political system'.[10]

The Macro-Referenced Behavior of the Legal Professionals

Defenders perceive that because D.A.s and judges are either elected or appointed by the Governor, both are influenced by 'political pressure'. Political pressure is exerted on these court officials by the 'public', a concept which translates more specifically into crime victims, the jury, the media, other lay members of the community as well as community sentiment and the electorate in general.[11] In face of a social environment that appears to emphasize law and order, this pressure is *not* to uphold defendants' civil rights but instead to convict[12] and punish them. On the other hand, Defenders discern that their own system of indigent defense has enabled them to provide highly ethical advocacy for criminal suspects.

The D.A.'s Conduct Robert described the macro-referenced behavior of D.A.s in the following comments:

> The District Attorney is an elected official. They are subject to public opinion. They are subject to political pressures. They are terrified of the press. And as a result, those factors bear on the organization of the District Attorney's office and they bring tremendous pressure to bear on individual Deputy District Attorneys. [Interviewer: To behave how?] It depends on the case, but usually to the detriment of the defendant, and usually to prosecute the case to the very fullest extent possible.

According to Defenders, because the District Attorney is elected by and accountable to the voters, he or she finds it necessary to present a good 'face' to the public. One major way in which he or she does this is by maintaining an impressive statistical record of convictions. This also means that the D.A. desires to settle as many cases as possible:

> Vera: Ideally, [Deputy D.A.s] dismiss a case if it's no good. But they do not do that in this D.A.'s office. They rarely dismiss a case. They'll make you some ridiculous offer, but they'll always get a conviction. And they're very, very concerned about statistics. And I'm sure you've heard this: they make their stats, they just want the conviction.

The Conduct of Judges Defenders do *not* perceive judges as neutral arbiters. Instead, because they too experience political pressure, they are said to favor the prosecution in rendering their decisions. However, judges are believed to experience some additional pressure from the D.A.'s office as well. This is illustrated in the following accounts:

> Ingmar: [Interviewer: Do you think judges experience any external pressure to behave particular ways?] Public opinion ... Not just public opinion. D.A.'s opinion. These days ... judges want to make sure that they're not seen as being soft ... especially when there's people in the courtroom – non-attorneys. They act tough and they are tough. [Interviewer: Why?] Because they don't want to be knocked out of position. And they have to run for office occasionally. And if they want to get into higher office with Governor _____, you can be assured that if you've got a reputation for being soft, you're not gonna be sent up to the appellate court if that's where you want to go.

> Kathy: The behavior of the judge is shaped by the same forces that work on the D.A.'s office. The general attitude, the public attitude of the police department, the public and private attitude of the D.A.'s office actually ... And then the judges are affected by the general law and order attitude of the community. [Interviewer: The reason?] Well, judges are up for election, too ... And they don't like to get criticized in the paper. And you don't see criticism in the paper for overly harsh sentences. What you see in the paper is judges getting criticized for giving someone probation when the press or the

media or the D.A.'s office is saying they should have got prison.

Also like D.A.s, judges are believed to experience pressure to settle cases. Unlike the D.A.'s office, however, this pressure is deemed to derive from the desire to conserve court resources. It is also viewed to ameliorate some of their bias toward prosecutors so that Defenders are able to obtain more concessions from judges during plea-bargaining than at other times.[13] One Defender gave the following explanation:

> William [In discussing plea-bargain negotiations]: Even when you actually get sent out to the Trial Department, judges are constantly putting pressure on the parties to resolve the cases. Serious cases. [Interviewer: Why?] Because there's so many of them and their calendars are so clogged. And just the great weight of all of that puts pressure on the judges, and of course they then hand that pressure over to the parties to settle ... I've seen judges take defense attorneys aside and tell them that their [client's] exposure [to sentences] will be higher if certain factors come out during the trial, if they don't plead, and kind of imply that they're gonna do a lot worse if they lose at trial than what they could get with this offer. [Interviewer: Do they make a similar threat to the D.A.?] Sure. There are threats they can make in the sense of, they could tell the D.A., 'Y'know from what I've heard, Mr. D.A. or Ms. D.A., if the facts of this case that come out in trial are the same ones that you and Mr. Defense Attorney have indicated to me here in chambers, I'm likely to give this guy probation. So if you think you're gonna go through this whole trial in the hopes that you're gonna get state prison from me, you're not gonna get it. Go back and talk to your supervisor – tell him that'. And he'll come back with a probation offer.

The Defenders' Conduct Many researchers have noted the ethical dilemmas in which certain organizational imperatives place defense attorneys. Blumberg (1967b) and Sudnow (1965), for example, argued that because criminal attorneys' careers hinge on cooperative relationships with the judge and the District Attorney, they are likely to sacrifice adversarial ideals. Blumberg also found that the private attorney's relationship with clients is structured around the fee: not only do they negotiate defendants' jail terms contingent on payment of the fee but defendants who pay greater fees receive more overall advocacy.[14]

While Defenders do not claim to have perfect relationships with their clients, consistent with numerous studies that indicate that defense attorneys for the poor perform at levels at least comparable to those of private attorneys,[15] neither do they claim that there is any organizational pressure that prohibits them from maintaining ethical relationships. In fact, most of them insist that aspects of their indigent defense organization actually facilitate their ability to provide good service to clients.[16] This is illustrated in the following comments:

> The Director [He was explaining the differences between this type of indigent defense organization and other types]: We are different from a contract office that's for profit. And I believe that it is the best of all possible worlds in that, on the one hand, your motivation is not profit, it's service, and people are encouraged to provide service ... [O]bviously they're concerned about what they're gonna make in terms of salary and such, but once that's taken care of, they can focus on their work. They don't have to worry about overhead or management of the office ... [In addition,] they're specialists and experts in their field and they focus completely on what I consider to be a very specialized area of the law ... [O]ur people are told to put in the amount of time that is necessary to properly represent the client. The case should not be disposed of or you should not go to trial based on economic concerns. That should be based on what's right for the client.

> LuAnn: [Clients] don't pay me by the hour. They don't pay me by the court hearing. So I can tell them the truth up front because my livelihood and my rent do not depend on whether I have this person as a client any longer than is necessary for this client.

> Nora: [Interviewer: Are you limited by your resources here?] We can get as much resources as we need. If we had more cases going to trial, we could get more resources. The county

would have to pay for it if we went to trial. It's just that they don't have the courtrooms and the judges to accommodate it

In addition, as Erlanger (1978), Katz (1982) and Platt and Pollock (1974) found with other attorneys for the poor, Defense Alliance appeared to attract into employment attorneys whose political ideologies and career aims were consistent with formal organizational goals. This is illustrated in the Defenders' responses to the question 'Why did you take a job with Defense Alliance?'

Ingmar: [Indigent defense has] always been the only thing I've really been interested in Law ... I refuse to work for certain organizations – for instance, I would never ever represent Exxon in anything ... And I don't want to work for some gigantic law firm where I'm working 75 hours per week to make somebody money. Why I want to do it is because I believe very strongly that people who are accused of crimes in this country are treated like hell, and that they deserve a good defense. And also I feel like I'm out there protecting everybody's rights by doing what I do. I know that the abuses that used to occur in the 1940s and 50s don't occur in the same way – they may occur occasionally in the same way, but the police aren't out there abusing people as much as they used to be. That's because people like me who came before me did these things.

Robert: 'Cause I'm interested in the Constitutional process. [Interviewer: Want to add anything?] Well, I'm interested in living in a free society. It's been said that criminal defense lawyers are the last champions of personal liberty.

Nora: Probably I would always gravitate toward this kind of work. I knew when I was in law school that I wanted to do something in poverty law. And this is poverty law. And I became aware at some point that I wanted to do trials ... I like helping the little guy as opposed to the big guy.

William: Well, I heard a lot of good things about [Defense Alliance]. That they were very professional, and they were hard fighters, I guess is one way to put it, took what they did seriously, and they were good litigators. And I wanted to become a better litigator. And I wanted to do felony work.

While the Defenders perceive that politics pressures D.A.s and judges to deal harshly with criminal suspects, they view themselves as guardians of the poor and powerless. This is consistent with McIntyre's (1987) assertion that the court system's need for legitimacy somewhat empowers public Defenders by enabling as well as encouraging them to assert their clients' rights. Additionally, it suggests that our political-legal system has institutionalized a contradiction whereby some segments of society feel compelled to accede to the dictates of the powerful while others are inspired to uphold the rights of the downtrodden.

The Macro-Referenced Behavior of the Non-Professionals

Recently, Nielsen (2000) found that the legal consciousness of ordinary citizens arises in part on the basis of their social location.[17] Similarly, Defenders apprehend that the behavior of juries, witnesses and indigent defendants is shaped by their 'social backgrounds', or, their somewhat unique political, economic, and cultural circumstances. These include such socioeconomic circumstances as occupation, education, race or ethnicity, wealth, place of residence, friend, kinship and intimacy networks, as well as personal history and experience. Overall, the divergent social backgrounds of these court actors indicate that while juries are not inclined to empathize with indigent defendants' situations, neither are indigent defendants typically equipped to convince the jury otherwise.

The Jury's Conduct   Due to the system for selecting the jury pool, the Defenders perceive that the typical jury in their jurisdiction is white, middle class and traditional if not conservative. They thereby conclude that the jury is predisposed to view reality quite differently from their clients.[18] This is evident in the following elaborations:

> Ingmar: If you're in downtown Smith City, the last jury I had there were a total of four blacks out of the 72 people called. And a couple of Hispanics. Five or six maybe. And then my two clients – one was black and one was Hispanic. If you're in downtown [another city], you get a lot more lower-class people and minorities of all sorts. And lower-class white people, too. Because juries are chosen from DMV records

and voter registration, you lose out on a lot of people ... [T]hey ought to add in all those people who get food stamps, and welfare, and we would see a lot more people on juries who were more the peers of our clients [Interviewer: What is the typical jury like in Smith City?] I would expect to find middle-class people who don't have much experience with the Law or with crime except for the fact that fifty percent of them have been burglarized, their homes have been burglarized and no one was ever caught.

Nora: [The typical jury is] Middle-class. Very different from our clients in lifestyle, experiences with the justice system, experience with crimes – they've never been accused of crimes usually, a little bit intimidated by the system, by lawyers, a little bit distrustful of the system. None of them are sure they trust the system or lawyers. The biggest problem I guess is that they're too far removed from our clients. I mean, our clients are not really judged by their peers, but another social strata up.

The Conduct of Witnesses Defenders perceive that the credibility of witnesses, including their likelihood of showing up at court hearings, is shaped by their political, economic and cultural backgrounds. To a large extent, this means that witnesses with high status are more likely to be viewed as credible. These discernments are apparent in the following comments:

Kathy: [Interviewer: How would you describe a good witness?] [T]he more middle-class your witness is, the more effective the testimony. The more articulate the witness is, the more effective the testimony. The more sophisticated or well-educated the witness is, the more effective his testimony is gonna be.

Ingmar: [Interviewer: How would you describe a good witness?] [Y]ou want people with backgrounds that are unimpeachable. Someone with a job. Depending on what it is, too, you want somebody who doesn't know your client ... Because he doesn't have any reason to lie. [Interviewer: What about status, in general?] Well, the better the social status of your client, the better off you are in general.

Mindy: [Interviewer: What are the methods by which you might seek to acquit a defendant?] Well, there are a number of ways. Sometimes it's just a matter of calling up to see if the complaining witness is still in town. If he's not, you just tell the D.A. that you don't want to plead ... and when the [prelim] date comes up, they don't have a witness and they have to dismiss the case. Lets say the victim is a Navy man; he may be out to sea. I hate to say this, but lets say it's a spousal abuse. A lot of times the victim is not gonna show up because a lot of times she loves him by the time the prelim comes around. And you know she's not gonna show up, so you don't take the offer.

The Conduct of Indigent Defendants As may also be surmised from some of the above comments, Defenders find that their clients are typically unable to assist adequately with their cases due to their marginal socioeconomic backgrounds. These perceptions are apparent in the following elaborations:

Mindy: ... usually if the person comes from the lower-economic scale, hand-in-hand with that seems to go lack of education. And therefore, we don't tend to have mental giants that we represent, and sometimes there's a stumbling block there because they don't quite grasp what you're trying to do for them, and they don't understand what the defense is or they don't quite know how to respond to questions by the D.A. or they can have whatever they say twisted around. Because they're not all that bright. That's part of it. I would say that's probably the main thing.

Robert: [Indigent defendants are] almost definitionally a member of the underclass. Which means that he is under or uneducated. Likely to be illiterate. He is typically inarticulate. He is often, usually a racial minority. All those things are important factors in how his case is gonna be heard and looked upon, and what the final determination is gonna be for his case ... The fact that a defendant is inarticulate limits his ability to get on the witness stand, and express himself to the jury. That goes hand in hand with his educational background. Members of the underclass have –

it is a subculture in which certain things are accepted, or tolerated which may not be tolerated by jurors who come from more of a mainstream kind of background.

Ingmar: I think in general they have a lot more difficult cases to defend. I mean there's certain things you don't have. You don't have wonderful character witnesses for them because you can't bring in all these members of the business community, and politics, and what have you to come in and testify that this person's character is unimpeachable.

Cultural Fluency

Throughout their routines, Defenders draw upon two overlapping cultural domains of meaning (or 'language systems') to make sense of their experiences and to communicate with others. These are 'legal expertise' and 'common sense'. They also expect other court actors to employ these cultural vernaculars to various degrees and in somewhat distinctive manners. Thus, court actors are seen to have diverse levels of *fluency* in these language systems. The discussion below describes legal expertise and common sense as well as the Defenders' expectations regarding their usage.

Legal Expertise

Ewick and Silbey use the term 'legal consciousness' to ' ... name participation in the process of constructing legality (1998:45)'. The construction of legality, in turn, is said to occur '[e]very time a person interprets some event in terms of legal concepts or terminology ... (1998:45)'. Clearly, legal consciousness and the construction of legality can be said to characterize the Defenders' behavior as well as that of other court actors. 'Legal expertise', however, refers not simply to legal consciousness and the construction of legality in general but moreover to *specialized* legal knowledge and productions.

'Legal expertise' is acquired through law school as well as participation in legal occupations, and is routinely brought to bear in formal negotiations of legal reality. It includes understandings not only of those laws and legal procedures enacted by legislators and Supreme Courts and then encoded in law books, but also of the somewhat unique practices and conditions of particular court jurisdictions.[19] It informs attorneys about such matters as what legal codes pertain in a case and the nuances of the courtroom work group.[20]

In essence, it includes everything about the law and legal system that the typical layperson would not know. Moreover and perhaps most importantly, it is the cultural arsenal upon which attorneys must draw to engage in their legal battles: it prescribes and circumscribes the range and types of weapons (i.e., the legal stories) that they may use to argue their cases.

The place and alleged necessity for fluency in the cultural idiom of legal expertise is illustrated in Defenders' responses to the question 'What makes you think the defendant needs an attorney such as you?'

> Ingmar: Because very few people out there have any idea of what it takes to represent themselves – in terms of going through a trial, in terms of plea bargaining, in terms of sentencing ... I mean they can get some Pro Per privileges, but they don't have the knowledge and the experience to defend someone ... And the District Attorney knows that when it comes to trial, they'll kick them all over the place. They don't know the law. And they're not about to learn it in the several months before trial.

> Kathy: A defendant not only needs a defense attorney. A defendant needs a defense attorney who's familiar with the criminal justice system. Familiar with the system through which the defendant is proceeding. Because – this may sound trite, but it's a jungle out there. Defendants who are not represented get hurt. People who are not represented in a knowledgeable way get hurt. They suffer the consequences. And, like I said, sometimes it's useful to have someone who knows the law and the legal issues – other than just the system.

> Steve: [T]he the defendant, no matter how smart he is, is going up against a trained prosecutor with three years of law school and whatever it took to pass the bar. Plus he's trained – he's in court all the time.

As apparent in the comments above, Defenders do not expect their clients to be fluent in legal expertise but instead to require the services of a professional. On the other hand, they not only expect all the attorneys to be fluent in this idiom but also to employ (or 'speak') it in a manner consistent with their roles. Thus, they anticipate that D.A.s will use this cultural vernacular in an effort to secure convictions and, as indicated in Karl's comments below, that judges will establish their decisions within it:

> It's amazing that the D.A. will give you years off sometimes the potential sentence [in striking a plea bargain], but the judge won't. And sometimes the judge can't ... *because of allegations, because of sentencing rules, sentencing laws ...* Where a D.A. can say, 'Well, we'll strike an allegation or this, that, and the other thing' and it puts you in a much more favorable position vis-à-vis sentencing. [Emphasis added.]

Although the jury consists of lay members of the community, ideally they are supposed to uphold the laws which judges provide them throughout a trial. However, Defenders maintain that most juries employ little or no legal expertise in their decision-making. Moreover, they complain that what little expertise jurors might employ is typically invoked to favor the prosecution. Thus, the jury is seen as legally naive, unskilled, unpredictable, and potentially dangerous.[21] This is apparent in LuAnn's and Kathy's comments:

> LuAnn: What I don't like about juries is that most of those people want to solve the case ... [T]hey don't really follow the jury instruction that says if there's two rational sides, and when one points to guilt and the other points to innocence, you're bound to find innocence. They much – if there's a flaw in the defense case, they'll hold it against the defense before they'll hold it against the prosecution.

> Kathy: They don't listen. They don't listen to the law. They go and do what they want to do. They shoot from the hip, is what I mostly see happening. And if you got somebody that they can put into their frame of reference and give them an explanation of their behavior that is suitable or acceptable to them, then they will go outside the law to acquit. But if you can't fit your particular client into that frame of reference, then they will not follow the law of reasonable doubt, circumstantial evidence.

Defenders expect all witnesses in criminal cases to possess and provide some 'special' and largely unshared knowledge. This is what makes them valuable *as* witnesses: unlike other court actors, they provide information regarding alleged crimes, alleged criminals, and/or other witnesses in a case which few or no other people can provide. They are not, however, necessarily expected to possess fluency in legal expertise. Those who do are commonly referred to as 'professional witnesses'. Unlike lay witnesses (who simply testify to the facts in a case) or expert witnesses (who provide interpretations of information from a specialized point of view), professional witnesses are proficient in the act of testifying itself: they know better than others both what to expect in front of a judge or jury, how to impress these court actors, and the best way to handle awkward situations presented to them while testifying. In essence, they are experts in legal rhetoric.

While professional witnesses may consist of investigators, doctors, and psychologists who are recurrently called upon to testify in cases, the most common are police officers, who Defenders believe are especially coached and trained by the D.A.[22] Thus, police officers are seen as formidable, frequent *as well as* extremely biased prosecution witnesses. As Tom explained,

> Police officer witnesses, you'll find, are experienced after a time. And some of them are very good. Some are superb witnesses. Best one I ever saw was a guy who had been a building contractor for years who got a job as an undercover police cop. He looked like Santa Claus. He was the most benevolent, warm, charming guy you ever met in your life. He got up there and lied his head off.

Common Sense

Also employed throughout the Defenders' routines is 'common sense'. According to Webster (1976), common sense is 'practical judgment or intelligence; ordinary good sense'. Sociologically and anthropologically, what is 'practical', 'intelligent', or 'good sense' is *cultural*. For example, it makes 'good sense' to us that if we want to survive in this society, we should find a job in order to make money. However, the very idea of 'jobs' or 'getting a job' is possible only within the context of relatively recent historical societies. A woman in a hunting and gathering society never fathomed the possibility of deciding whether she should become a 'gatherer' in order to make a living and survive. It was simply understood that this was who she was born to be and that this was how she would contribute to group survival.

Consequently, common sense is better defined as the shared stock of knowledge in a society or the core understandings that most people in a specific cultural community hold in common.[23] It enables people in a large society to interact meaningfully by providing them with a set of shared, taken-for-granted understandings that form the context for communication. It also prescribes what is *and is not* expected, normal and acceptable behavior in the cultural community. For example, in developed western societies, we know how to behave as well as how people *should* behave in a store, a library, and a hospital. Such understandings are not possible in societies where stores, libraries and hospitals do not exist and members of such societies do not know how to behave 'appropriately' in such contexts. Yet common sense is not knowledge about which we typically think or talk. Instead, it is tacitly understood and taken-for-granted. In other words, it makes our everyday communication possible, but it is rarely acknowledged as anything worth talking about.

As Gusfield (1981) finds, common sense also entails recognition of the conventional social hierarchy and structure of authority. In our developed, western society, for example, scientific spheres of activity are implicitly accorded more legitimacy than enterprises in such mystical domains as astrology.[24] We also have more respect for scientists than business people, and treat the latter with more deference than prostitutes. Yet it is important to realize that such collective sentiments are not culturally or historically invariant: scientists have been regarded as heretics, merchants have been despised, and prostitutes have had high status in other societies.[25] Consequently, *common sense should be seen as the shared values, beliefs and norms of the status quo in particular societies.*

Regardless of whether they themselves wholly embrace common sense, Defenders assume that judges and juries do. As noted earlier, juries are considered middle class and without empathy for poor defendants. Similarly, judges are deemed extremely sensitive to public opinion and social proprieties due to their roles as elected officials. Thus, judges and juries are generally regarded as social conformists who sustain conventional viewpoints, or, the viewpoints of the status quo. In effect, they *are* the status quo.[26]

Kathy's description of one motion hearing illustrates that Defenders expect judges to employ common sense in their decision-making:

> [In a] normal [search and seizure motion], you're trying to show [the judge] that there was an illegal search and seizure, that is, a search or seizure that occurred without probable cause ... [Interviewer: Can you give me an example?] The case in City Park. First of all, the police officer was lying about where he was, where he said he was. And so we had photographs of where the police officer said he was to

demonstrate the fact that nobody in the world would have conducted a dope deal right in front of him. And that even if he was where he said he was, *he could not have seen what he said he saw. He could not have seen the transaction occur.* [Emphasis added.]

As these comments reveal, Defenders expect judges to assume – given the commonly shared understanding of one objective and intersubjective world[27] – that people cannot be in two places at one time. Therefore, because a police officer stated that he was at a place whereby no single person could have seen what he said he witnessed, the Defender expected the judge to conclude that the police officer was lying.

Nevertheless, because of their politically sensitive positions, Defenders expect judges to render decisions that favor the prosecution. Thus, they expect judges to maintain a more conservative stance toward what constitutes 'reasonable', persuasive or sufficient defense evidence. As Kathy continued to explain,

[I]t feels like the standard [of proof for defense motions] is much higher than ['by a preponderance of the evidence'] ... It feels ... like a *much* higher standard – basically you have to prove, you have to show the court [i.e., judge] that the officer could not have seen what he or she said they saw. That it *could not* have happened the way that officer said. Beyond a reasonable doubt and to a moral certainty – actually it feels like, with some judges, beyond all possible doubt.

Consistent with Kalven and Zeisel's (1976) findings, Defenders do not expect the jury to be as conviction-oriented as D.A.s and judges. However, they *are* expected to employ common sense from a similar viewpoint, a *traditional* one. This is apparent in Kathy's comments:

Kathy (She had earlier alluded to 'the right frame of reference' for juries.): [Interviewer: What is the 'right frame of reference' for the jury?] I had a client – a cute little white kid who was 22, and he was charged with battery on his wife's lesbian lover. Well, now, all I had to do – there was a fight and he told the lesbian lover to get out of the house, and she basically told him to fuck off, and so he threw her out.

> And I think technically he was guilty of a battery. But all I had to do was give the jury something they could use to acquit him with, and they did. [Interviewer: What did you give them?] A jury instruction; something to the effect that one has the right to ... use force to remove a trespasser from the house. And I saw their faces [light up] when they heard that jury instruction ... Now it's hard for a jury – if you've got a crime that none of them can really feel strong about, negatively ... Even though the person is not guilty, *technically* not guilty, jurors do not like to acquit in those cases. If I can't put the act into some kind of frame of reference to make it acceptable. [Interviewer: Behaving on the basis of certain traditional values?] Right. [Interviewer: One is that a woman shouldn't have a lesbian lover?] Right. [Interviewer: And the other one is that, sort of working-class, conservative type values?] I don't know if they're working-class, conservative, but yeah, I know what you mean. Yes, traditional values.

Because it is the cultural framework with which judges and juries are believed to interpret behavior, witnesses are seen to employ the rhetoric of common sense whether or not they do so intentionally. Their level of fluency in this idiom varies, however. And it varies in conjunction with their level of credibility. In general, the principle in operation here is that the more a witness's cultural rhetoric is consistent with the judge and jury's commonsense standards and beliefs (or the norms and values of the status quo), the more credible (or persuasive) she or he is expected to be.[28]

One may question the validity of the latter insofar as expert witnesses provide information not easily understood by judging authorities and yet strike observers as generally more credible than lay witnesses. However, it is important to keep in mind that the actual 'testimony' witnesses provide consists of verbal and non-verbal as well as blatant and subtle messages. Apart from their oral statements regarding an incident, for example, witnesses are always introduced at the beginning of their attestations with such prefatory information as their name, occupation, and with regard to expert witnesses, credentials. Additionally, witnesses speak and comport themselves in more or less socially acceptable or desirable manners. All of these messages may be more or less consistent with traditional interpretations of commonsense proprieties. Thus, expert witnesses typically provide 'testimony' which fits better into a commonsense framework than that delivered by lay witnesses.

For example, one witness's identification as an undercover police officer in the case described below 'explained' in a taken-for-granted manner not only why he was (legitimately) privy to a drug deal, but also why he would be viewed as more credible than the defendant, who was alleged to be not only a drug dealer but also a convicted child molester:[29]

> Tom: [In]one [case] I was talking to you about before lunch, where the guy was charged with child molest [previously] and then he sold a couple of kilos of cocaine to some undercover cop and an informant, the only defense we could have in that case was an entrapment defense. Saying that this guy had basically been set up by these two people, and it was gonna be difficult. And one of the things that I had to take into consideration and counsel him about was the fact that the only way if we took this case to trial that we could ever possibly win was with him testifying ... One of the things that was gonna come out was the fact that he had this 288 – this child molest prior. That's not something that would have endeared him to the jury. Now it's conceivable that we might have been able to sanitize that prior in the sense that the prosecutor would have been able to ask him only if he had been convicted of a felony and not what it was. But then again the jury would think, 'Well, gee whiz. If he's been convicted of a felony, it was probably a drug offense or something like that' and use it against him anyway.

Similarly, the Defenders' comments below illustrate not simply that witnesses' physical appearances are thought to send more or less persuasive messages to judging authorities but moreover that the consistency of this rhetoric with traditional commonsense expectations is expected to evoke positive assessments of credibility:

> Mindy: [Interviewer: How would you describe a good witness?] [T]here are plenty of times I've said, 'Gee, I wish I could have' – its kind of a joke, y'know – 'a pinch defendant'. Let somebody else sit in on this guy because this guy looks so terrible. He just looks like a guilty person. [Interviewer: Can you give me an example?] Well, somebody that looks like a thug, maybe. Some great big burly looking guy that you'd be afraid to walk down the alley

with at night. And if he's accused of robbery, automatically the jury is gonna look at the guy and say that guy looks like a robber ... And he's got all kinds of strikes against him before he ever takes the stand and opens his mouth.

Steve: [Interviewer: When you were discussing defendants, what did you mean by 'presentable'?] Basically means that the jury can relate to that person as compared to thinking of him as some other category of person. If you have an all white jury, middle-class such as I came up against in Federal Court, and you have a minority client that has nothing in common with the jurors, then they're less likely to open their hearts to that person or their minds aren't open to the argument that you're making on their behalf. You have a much more difficult time selling your version of the case to that trier of fact, the body of jurors.

Ingmar (He had previously mentioned 'well-dressed' as one characteristic of a good witness.): [Interviewer: What do you mean by 'well-dressed'?] I mean dressed in clean clothes, not a T-shirt that says 'bull-shirt' on it. I always tell my witnesses and my client to wear a suit if you're a male ... that's the best. Because most people in my opinion, have a prejudice and they tend to equate that with – I don't know the word, but it just seems to work. A woman, just nice – the kind of clothes that you'd come in to a job interview. Something like that. Conservative.

As stated earlier, because the judge and jury decide crucial issues between the prosecution and defense, Defenders conduct much of their legal practice with these actors in mind. This means that most if not all of their advocacy is founded in the cultural vernacular of common sense:

Doug (He was explaining to the researcher how to write a statement of mitigation for a defendant): You know what common law is, don't you? It's all based on common sense. That's what a lawyer does. He does things based on common sense.

Nora: The legal expertise is the rules, the building blocks that – the confines within which you have to work. The law says you have to do it 'this way' ... Within that [framework], you try to use your people skills ... [Interviewer: How about common sense?] ... That's part of people skills. You have to be able to read people. Figure out what's gonna work for a trial – make people believe that, if possible.

Karl: [During a jury trial,] I cast doubt on anything that I can find. Now you don't do overkill in terms of manufacturing stupid theories. [Interviewer: Like what?] Well, I don't know. Maybe that your client didn't really enter the house and take out the microwave, that the family dog next door did ... [Y]ou try to find things that seem to be casting doubt, and that doubt is based upon some kind of reason, *some kind of common sense* that jibes with the facts of your case. [Emphasis added.]

Unfortunately, while the Defenders' advocacy is grounded largely in the cultural idiom of common sense, indigent defendants are not typically fluent in this vernacular. Instead, they are apt to present themselves and their criminal cases through a less persuasive, culturally disparate rhetoric. This is explained in the following comments:

LuAnn: Many times [defendants do not testify] because they simply do not present well in court. They do not tell their story well. They either do not understand the game plan well enough ... Or they simply don't speak well. A lot of times, we're dealing with somebody from a bad neighborhood, totally alien environment – to bring them into the court system and expect them to dress up in a suit and tie is ridiculous. I've had to clothe more clients than not. And then to expect them to comport themselves properly, and what is proper is what the judge and jury think are proper.

William: Well, I would say that they live in another world. Typically, a world where everybody's poor. A world where police, for the most part, are not your friends. Where all your family and friends are involved with crime or are on the fringes of crime. Where your trust of establishment types is usually very low because they usually try to incarcerate you or take advantage of you, or at least they treat you in a different fashion because you're not familiar with their world.

Nora: [The average non-indigent defendant would] probably have presentable witnesses who come and speak on his behalf ... The more unlike an indigent defendant, the more ideal they are. The less poor they look and act, and sound because it's easier to present that person to jurors ... I had an ideal client once who graduated from college, was first in her class. The Dean of the college bailed her out of jail when she got arrested.

Conclusion

In their seminal studies on criminal defense attorneys, Sudnow (1965) and Blumberg (1967a) characterized publicly provided lawyers as types of bureaucratic functionaries of the court system whose primary role is to facilitate guilty pleas and conviction rates.[30] Consistent with more recent findings,[31] this study shows that, in contrast, the Defenders maintain an adversarial stance toward their task. This orientation is encouraged by the cultural context in which they anticipate their duties. Specifically, while role prerequisite behaviors somewhat institutionalize the norm of conflict implicit in our adversarial system of justice, additional opposition is brought about through macro-referenced behavior whereby Defenders attempt to restrain other court actors' potential abuse of power by defending the Constitution. The attorneys' legal expertise then becomes a cultural resource upon which they draw to fight their legal battles.

As a result, it appears that poor defendants' economic status has no negative effect and perhaps a positive effect on the Defenders' motivation to perform their task ethically. Yet this does not mean that indigent suspects are unlikely to endure any other inequities in the adjudication of their cases.

The role prerequisite behaviors discussed here can be seen to bring about a set of relationships whereby some people are accorded the authority to judge others. This set of relationships does not in itself dictate that social class intervenes, however. Instead, class biases are introduced through macro-referenced conduct that is expressed through the cultural idiom of common sense, a language system with which all actors are expected to make meaning yet one in which indigent defendants are not very fluent. In essence, the judge and jury are found to uphold status quo standards of respectability and credibility in cases involving defendants who, almost by definition, are typically unable to live up to such standards. Thus, the Defenders encounter numerous difficulties in attempting to build viable defense rhetoric for their clients and poor defendants are apt to endure inequities because litigation procedures involve *commonsense 'class'ism*, or, unequal treatment on the basis of social class that derives from commonsense reasoning.

These findings are consistent with many of those generated by other scholars who have sought to understand the impact of social class on adjudication outcomes. Employing positivist methodologies, for example, some researchers have found that a defendant's social class effects case outcomes in association with some type of stereotype[32] or as social characteristics that elicit sympathy from middle-class judges and jurors.[33] A number of interpretive scholars have additionally found that such images are not static but are instead *actively compiled* by court actors[34] and reflect cultural images and stereotypes.[35] The key distinction of the findings presented here is the emphasis placed on the role of common sense as both a widely shared cultural context and an idiom used, on the one hand, to defend poor criminal suspects and, on the other hand, to oppress the very same persons.

Notes

1   See Mehan and Wood (1975) and Pollner (1974).
2   Although not envisioned as role prerequisite behaviors Neubauer (1974) described the same role behaviors for defense attorneys in Prairie City.
3   See also the guidelines for ethical conduct prescribed by the American Bar Association (1986).
4   All names are pseudonyms. Indented excerpts are transcripts of taped interviews. Because this is not a conversational analysis, however, the researcher has omitted such things as silences, overlapping talk as well as nonessential repetitive or digressive comments (These are noted by ellipses). Information in brackets refers either to interviewer comments (as noted), to information which has been translated from the Defenders' somewhat opaque argot (e.g., references to a '459' has been translated into 'burglary' where appropriate), or to other contextual information necessary to understand certain comments.
5   See for example, Neubauer (1974) and Wice (1985).
6   This is consistent with Wice's (1985) conclusions regarding the prosecutor's role in sixteen different cities.
7   It is important to note, however, that while Smith City judges will decide on the evidence in preliminary and motion hearings, they do not do that in trials. There are no judge trials in this jurisdiction.

8   Except that this study focuses on defense attorneys, this behavior is consistent with Emerson and Paley's (1992) finding that prosecutors maintain a 'downstream orientation' toward cases. See also Frohmann (1991; 1997).

9   See also Frohmann (1997), Mather (1979) and Maynard (1984a).

10 Silbey (1992) makes a similar observation of how macro structures are constituted in everyday practice and have a place in the cultural analysis of law.

11 With regard to judges, see also the findings of Danet and Bogoch (1980) and Drechsel (1987). See Pritchard (1986) for a discussion regarding the effect of crime news on prosecutors' decisions to plea bargain cases and Farr (1984) for a discussion regarding the effect of certain policies in the DA's office on plea-bargaining.

12 With regard to prosecutors' behavior (see also the findings of Frohmann (1991), Pritchard (1986), Stanko (1982) and Wice (1985).

13 In keeping with Uhlman and Walker's (1980) findings about the judiciary's behavior in a major eastern community, the pressure that Smith City judges exert on attorneys to settle cases is primarily sentencing pressure.

14 For further examples, see Alschuler (1975), Aprile (1986), Carlin (1962), Guggenheim (1986), Irons (1983), Platt and Pollock (1974) and Underwood (1986).

15 See for example (Hermann et al. (1977), Mather (1979), McIntyre (1987), Wheeler and Wheeler (1980) and Wice (1985).

16 For more details regarding how this unique defense organization appears to facilitate an ethnical defense posture, see Emmelman (1993).

17 See also Ewick and Silbey (1998).

18 Frohmann (1997) makes a similar observation with regard to prosecutors. Similarly, the findings of Deosaran (1984), Feild (1978), Johnson (1985) and Kalven and Zeisel (1976) all indicate that some aspect of jurors' backgrounds influence their verdicts.

19 This latter aspect of legal expertise appears to correspond most closely to what Church (1982) calls 'local legal culture'.

20 The significance of the courtroom work group for legal negotiations was first brought to our attention by Eisenstein and Jacob (1977). For examples of such nuances, see Eisenstein, Flemming and Nardulli (1988), Eisenstein and Jacob (1977), and Ulmer (1996).

21 See also the findings of Mather (1979) and Neubauer (1974). For studies that examine the extent to which this may actually be true, see Kalven and Zeisel (1976), Myers (1979) and Reskin and Visher (1986).

22 This belief is consistent with Cloyd's (1975) findings.

23 See for example, Berger and Luckmann (1967), Geertz (1983), Mehan and Wood (1975) and Schutz (1962). It should be noted here that the term as used in this analysis is not intended to denote that set of understandings which is shared only by the regular participants in a court system (see for example, Maroules, 1986). Instead it parallels the set of cultural or cognitive understandings that Gusfield (1981) calls 'public consciousness'. According to Gusfield, public consciousness refers to the ways in which the regular participants in a large cultural community conceptualize and manage problems and other phenomena. It is the cognitive order of society. Gusfield, however, is concerned with the ordered ways in which ideas and activities emerge in the public arena as problems whereas common sense refers here to an already structured public consciousness, or a public consciousness in which overt conflict is relatively absent and the ideas and ways of conceptualizing phenomena are taken-for-granted. This also appears to be the manner in which Stanko (1982) and Frohmann (1991) have conceptualized common sense in their studies on victim assessment.

24 See also, Weber (1979).

25 See for examples, Reston (1995), Sanger (1974) and Weber (1958).

26 It is also important to point out here that LaFree's (1985b) findings on Hispanic defendants emphasize the need to consider varying cultural contexts of commonsense. Again, common sense should be seen as the values, beliefs and norms of the status quo and since the status quo varies somewhat from place to place, so will the specific values, beliefs and norms used to judge and sentence defendants. Miller (1987) can be seen to make a similar point in her study of sentencing and inequality as a property of communities.

27 See Pollner (1974).

28 This appears to be completely consistent with Conley and O'Barr's (1998) findings regarding law, language and power. Ewick and Silbey (1995) also make a similar observation regarding the role of hegemony in narrative. The difference here appears to be a matter of emphasis, which in this analysis is on the taken-for-granted cultural context of common sense.

29 This case also illustrates that being identified as a person with a criminal record implies credibility problems. As discussed in later chapters, it is in this manner that a label or stigma associated with a formal finding of guilt most strongly affects Defenders' negotiations of convictions for crime.

30 For similar depictions of publicly provided defense attorneys, see Alschuler (1975; 1986), Guggenheim (1986), Lerner (1986), Nelson (1988) and Platt and Pollock (1974).

31 See for example, Feeley (1979), Flemming (1986), Hermann et al (1977), Heumann (1975), Mather (1979), McDonald (1985), McIntyre (1987), Neubauer (1974), Rosett and Cressey (1976), Skolnick (1967), Wheeler and Wheeler (1980) and Wice (1985).

32 E.g., Farrell (1971) and Swigert and Farrell (1977).

33 E.g., Kruttschnitt (1980). In contrast, see Reskin and Visher (1986).

34 In his study of defendant attributes in plea-bargaining, Maynard (1982) finds that legal professionals *assemble* images of defendants contingent upon the purpose-at-hand and from a number of potential attributes. Thus, he emphasizes the importance of considering ' ... defendant's attributes as elements selectively and contextually assembled in a specific gestalt for each case (:358)'. Like Maynard, other interpretive scholars have considered how social class influences case processing through images that are compiled by various court actors. In her study of skid row alcoholics, Wiseman (1979) found that middle class judges sentence individuals found guilty of public drunkenness on the basis of certain social characteristics that are objectified into social types. The more these social characteristics (which include the defendant's social position, past performance, and general physical appearance) conform to the values and standards of middle-class judges, the more likely a defendant will receive a lenient sentence from the judge. Similarly, in her study on prosecutorial decision-making, Frohmann (1997) discusses how these attorneys construct and employ 'discordant locales' to justify case rejection. 'Discordant locales' are an interweaving of person and place descriptions whereby jurors and victims are portrayed as members of geographically and culturally separate places. They are used to 'explain' the problems prosecutors anticipate that this situation will cause for obtaining convictions. In addition, in constructing discordant locales, prosecutors constitute the moral character of juror and victim residents as well as reproduce ideologies of race and class in the criminal justice system. Finally, in his study of insurance denials, Glenn (2000) finds that while formal narratives emphasize actuarial tables, subjective underwriting guidelines emphasize character assessment. The rationale for such underwriting is to avoid insuring 'moral hazards'. However, in making character assessments, underwriters employ seemingly objective criteria that recapitulate the lifestyles of less moneyed group members. Glenn

argues that the problem with this is that such standards do not necessarily predict *actual* moral hazards but instead merely penalize persons on the basis of their social class.

35 See for example, Frohmann (1991), Holstein (1993), Loeske (1992) and Matoesian (1995).

Chapter Three

Plea Bargain or Trial?
Assessing the Value of a Case

Numerous researchers have debated whether attorneys' decisions to plea bargain cases entail the sacrifice of justice ideals. As suggested in Chapter One, instead of legal considerations, publicly provided lawyers are said to base their decisions on such extra-legal factors as high case loads and inadequate funding,[1] the need to maintain cooperative relationships with other members of the court system,[2] the desire to maximize income,[3] political co-option,[4] and social class.[5] In contrast, other investigators have argued that legal variables play a fundamental role in this decision-making. They have found, for example, that the strength of evidence, the defendant's prior record, and the seriousness of a crime are crucial considerations and that defense attorneys advise their clients to plea-bargain when it means less serious penalties than those that are likely to be incurred after a trial.[6]

The findings reported here are consistent with those of the latter observers. Specifically, Defenders assess whether a case should be plea bargained or taken to trial on the basis of its 'value'. The 'value' of a case reflects Defenders' 'downstream' concerns regarding convictability and the potential penalties a defendant might incur after a trial.[7] It is determined by considering the seriousness of the crime, the strength of the evidence, and the defendant's background. Together, these factors indicate what the D.A. will probably offer the defendant for a guilty plea and whether he or she might be better off accepting it rather than proceeding to trial.[8] A case with little value is associated with high costs for pleading guilty (i.e., it is not worth much in terms of reduced penalties) and one with great value is associated with little cost (i.e., the prosecutor is apt to offer the defendant substantially reduced penalties for pleading guilty).

In assigning values to cases, Defenders must gauge the strength of evidence, evaluate the defendant's background, and then estimate the cost of plea-bargaining. This chapter examines the details of these calculations.

Gauging the Strength of Evidence

Defenders gauge the strength of evidence through a tacit, taken-for-granted process that emulates trial proceedings: based on their implicit understanding of evidence, they envision a courtroom dialogue wherein the prosecution and defense take turns presenting their cases in front of a judge and jury. At issue throughout the dialogue is whether or to what extent information is sufficient, legal and persuasive enough to convict the defendant.

The discussion below first describes the Defenders' general and largely unspoken understanding of evidence. It then describes precisely how Defenders assess information that could be presented at court hearings in light of this understanding.

The Defenders' Understanding of 'Evidence': A Format for Legal Story-Telling

The Defenders' understanding of evidence is established by and acquired through interaction with their legal community. Although they originally developed this understanding at law school, it has become somewhat modified and ingrained throughout their routine practice of law. It constitutes part of their unspoken 'legal expertise'. It is also held in common to some extent with other court actors.[9]

As defined by one leading authority, evidence in the legal community is

> any species of proof, or probative matter, legally presented at
> the trial of an issue by the act of the parties and through the
> medium of witnesses, records, documents, concrete objects,
> etc., for the purpose of inducing belief in the minds of the
> court or jury as to their contention (Black, 1968: 656).

As this definition indicates, the concept of evidence contains all the ingredients of trial proceedings: it encompasses the use of opposing attorneys, witnesses, judges, juries and physical objects, as well as laws dictating the issues and processes of litigation. Along with jury trials, it subsumes preliminary and motion hearings. All these ingredients have import in the Defenders' understanding of evidence. In essence, evidence to them is *any information which is lawfully presented to convince judging authorities that a specific contention regarding a criminal matter is true or, in defense at criminal trials, in doubt.* As such, it can also be seen as *a type of narrative or story-telling that conforms to a specific format.*[10] As Amsterdam and Bruner state,

> In litigation, the plaintiff's lawyer is required to tell a story in
> which there has been trouble in the world that has affected

the plaintiff adversely and is attributable to the acts of the defendant. The defendant must counter with a story in which it is claimed that nothing wrong happened to the plaintiff (or that the plaintiff's conception of wrong does not fit the law's definition), or, if there has been a legally cognizable wrong, then it is not the defendant's fault. Those are the obligatory plots of the law's adversarial process (2000: 117).

In the Smith County criminal court, the format for evidentiary narrative or story-telling is prescribed through three interrelated dimensions along which Defenders assess the viability of evidence prior to plea-bargaining. These are 1) sufficiency, 2) legality, and 3) persuasiveness.

'Sufficiency' means that Defenders perceive evidentiary story-telling in a quasi-scientific manner; i.e., it must not merely be adequate, but must be able to substantiate fully a hypothesis, with untainted, unbiased information, by some standard of proof before judging authorities. Rather than a law of nature, however, evidence is used to test or prove one or more hypotheses related to a defendant's guilt. The judging authorities who must be convinced of the accuracy of the contention also differ from those in the scientific community: while colleagues judge the evidentiary stories constructed and presented by scientists, judges and lay members of the community appraise the stories put forth by attorneys. Nevertheless, both scientists and attorneys systematically present information in order to test or prove hypotheses.

Like scientific evidence, evidence stories in the legal arena also entail the use of certain standards of proof regarding the acceptance and rejection of hypotheses. The scientific community employs such standards as $P<.05$, for example, while the criminal court community employs the standard of proof 'beyond a reasonable doubt'.

As discussed earlier, juries are the principal judges of information during trials in Smith City. (There are no bench trials for felony cases in their jurisdiction.) Although the jury is not expected to understand the intricacies of the criminal code and legal procedures, the judge is expected to possess such knowledge, and because he or she instructs the jury, monitors trials, as well as appraises evidence in other proceedings, the Defenders pay close attention to legal details and the procedures for presenting evidence.

All the Defenders displayed an awareness of the dimension of sufficiency throughout their everyday routines. Specifically, all of them at some time throughout the study revealed the understanding not merely that the prosecutor must prove the defendant's guilt, but more precisely that the prosecutor must

1) for every crime lodged against the defendant, 2) prove beyond a reasonable doubt, 3) with information legally obtained and presented (i.e., with untainted, unbiased data), 4) that every element of a specific crime as defined by the state's penal code occurred, and 5) that the defendant committed each crime alleged. Anything other than this suggested to them that the prosecution could not document all or part of its case and that one or more 'null' hypotheses regarding the defendant's guilt should be accepted.

Despite this understanding, Defenders were not wholly attentive to every aspect of sufficiency throughout *all* their routines. In fact, it was only during jury trials that Defenders were observed contesting techniques for presenting evidence or arguing that the prosecution had not proven their case 'beyond a reasonable doubt'. Otherwise, this dimension was most apparent during settlement hearings wherein it was common for a Defender to claim that the D.A. could not document that some element of a crime occurred in a particular case.

For example, in one case of battery against a police officer (where intent is an element of the crime), the Defender explained to the judge during a settlement conference that the defendant did not *intend* to hurt a police officer. He argued that instead the defendant was simply trying to escape and that the police officer got in the way of the defendant's retreating car. The judge quickly concluded, 'It's not a battery!' and encouraged the prosecutor to reconsider her initial offer. Although reluctant to offer a more palatable plea bargain, the prosecutor conceded that the judge and the Defender's assessment was correct and that (in essence) the prosecution narrative did not conform to the proper story-telling format.

Similarly, in another case where a defendant was found sleeping without permission in a stranger's home, the Defender argued that the defendant desired only a safe place to sleep and did not *intend to commit theft or some other felony*. Because this intent is a necessary element of the crime of burglary (or an essential component of a burglary story), he insisted that the defendant committed only the crime of trespass. The charge against the defendant was later reduced to comply with the Defender's demands.

The dimension of 'legality' means that evidence must fall within expressly *legal* guidelines. This dimension requires Defenders to think more like attorneys than scientists. In the criminal court, three major types of law define pertinent legal guidelines. These are penal codes (which define specific crimes and precisely what must be shown in order to prove that a crime was committed), 'Rules of Evidence' (which govern the content of admissible evidence) as well as Constitutional Law (which governs the procedures by which evidence can be obtained or presented). These laws are enmeshed and embodied in statutory and case law at both federal and state levels.

As discussed in Chapter Two, the Defenders expect all judges and attorneys involved in their cases to be aware of appropriate legal guidelines. However, they also believe opposing attorneys have quite different interests at stake. In particular, while the District Attorney is ideally responsible for upholding the law and executing justice, prosecutors (as well as police) are thought to harbor an inordinate desire to convict defendants. On the other hand, Defenders consider it their responsibility to protect defendants' rights. Consequently, they assume the prosecution will attempt to present information that does not actually comply with the law (or follow the appropriate format for legal story-telling), and that any information the defense hopes to present will be scrutinized very carefully as well.

Legality was clearly identified as part of the blueprint for evidentiary story-telling when Defenders questioned police officers' reports concerning procedures for searching suspects and making arrests. One Defender, for example, wondered aloud whether a police officer was lying or actually saw a packet of cocaine lying beside a suspect before searching him. Similarly, after timing a run from a kitchen to a bathroom and then to a front door, another Defender doubted whether a police officer had actually given a defendant ample time to respond to a knock before breaking down a door. Regardless of the truth in either case, their questioning presupposed the understanding that police officers do not *legally* have free rein to search suspects and that a judge should not permit information obtained outside these laws (or narratives that do not conform to the prescribed story-telling format) to be admitted as evidence.[11]

'Persuasiveness' means that evidence is made up of phenomena used to recount and reconstruct incidents in order to convince others of a contention: Whether animate or inanimate, verbal or nonverbal, evidence sends messages and evokes meaning that sways others' perceptions, opinions and judgments. Evidence is therefore symbolic and can be understood only within the framework of a cultural domain of meaning. As such, it also constitutes what Kenneth Burke (1989) calls 'rhetoric' which is subject to the constraints of social actors' cultural 'grammar'. The persuasive dimension of evidence requires that Defenders think like public speakers such as politicians, and the primary cultural domain with which Defenders assess persuasiveness is 'common sense'.

Persuasiveness, as a dimension of evidentiary story-telling based upon common sense, was apparent in one incident involving an arson case. The Defender was preparing for a sentencing hearing and stated that although the defendant insisted he was innocent, she and the victim both believed he was guilty. They concluded this because the defendant, presuming powers of ESP, stated to the victim during a visit that he 'sensed' a fire. The defendant was correct even though he was not in a physical position to actually see the victim's car on fire. The defendant's claims that he also possessed other supernatural attributes further convinced the Defender that he was mentally unstable – a claim she intended to invoke during the sentencing hearing.

This example illustrates the Defenders' view that scientific narratives of behavior (e.g., psychological accounts) are more consistent with common sense in our society and therefore more believable than supernatural accounts. It also suggests that when supernatural or other less legitimate versions of reality contradict or threaten social customs, the Defenders may completely discount their validity as well as their viability as evidentiary narratives.

Another Defender in a case involving automobile theft discerned the persuasive dimension of evidence. The defendant maintained that he did not know he was driving a stolen car. The Defender insisted that because the ignition switch was broken and dangling down the front of the dashboard while the defendant was driving the car, no jury would ever believe his story. She reasoned that the jury would think that the defendant 'had' to know something was 'obviously' wrong with the car. Interestingly (and sadly) enough, the defendant was from a very poor region of another country where it was apparently normal for cars to be driven with broken, punched-out ignition switches. However, because his account was incongruous with mainstream culture (or the commonsense values, beliefs and norms assumed to be maintained by the jury), the Defender deemed it unpersuasive and an inadequate evidence story.

A number of scholars have observed that a person's social characteristics or status influence the processing of criminal cases either directly (e.g., as judges, jurors or witnesses in a trial) or indirectly (e.g., through such variables as bail release and type of attorney).[12] The findings reported here support these research conclusions. However, they further indicate that social status acquires significance in criminal cases insofar as it shapes (or does *not* shape) the persuasiveness of 'facts' understood as actual or potential evidence. Unlike a business person or teacher, for example, common sense dictates that a homeless person has an incentive to steal as well as a consequent motive to lie about it. Thus, a homeless person who denies committing theft is inherently less persuasive than a business person or teacher who does the same. In addition, because he or she is unlikely to have other socially acceptable accouterments (such as a job, strong family ties, or reputable character witnesses), a person with low status is less able than persons with higher status to present convincing facts during a trial to contest an issue. A homeless person cannot, for example, claim that she was working or at home with family members during the time period in which a crime was committed. Moreover, what information he or she has to present may not be convincing from the standpoint of common sense, or the values, beliefs and norms of the status quo.[13] If the local drug addict who lives on the street or in nearby low-income housing vouches for the defendant, for example, the jury may find that testimony unbelievable, if not find greater fault with a defendant.[14] Thus, it is not a person's social status *alone* that effects his or her case, but the social conditions associated with his or her status, how or whether those conditions enter as evidentiary facts in the case, and most importantly, how convincing those facts are within the cultural framework of common sense.[15]

As stated earlier, Defenders gauge the strength of evidence prior to plea bargaining through a tacit, taken-for-granted process that emulates trial proceedings. This process consists of three stages. They are 1) assessing the prosecutor's case against the defendant (wherein Defenders consider what story the prosecutor will present during court hearings), 2) building and assessing a potential defense case (wherein Defenders consider how they might respond to prosecution claims and construct an alternative account), and 3) weighing the evidence (wherein Defenders conclude the dialogue by balancing defense and prosecution claims to determine whether or to what extent the prosecution can 'prove' their allegations). Throughout the process, Defenders appraise stories presented to them as potential evidence by considering whether they conform to the appropriate format; specifically, by determining whether they are sufficient, legal, and persuasive accounts. The details of this process are described below.

Assessing the D.A.'s Evidence Against the Defendant

The first thing Defenders generally do upon receiving a case is read it. The file contents usually include the 'complaint' (a list of the criminal counts with which the defendant is charged), an information sheet (a sheet usually filled-out by the defendant him or herself which lists such information as his or her name, address, telephone number, education, place of employment, and a little social history), a C.I.P. sheet (a form filled-out by Central Intake Personnel at the jail which lists, in addition to the above information, any priors or outstanding warrants and a recommendation for bail), and all the 'discovery' (i.e., all the information relating to any evidence which the D.A. will be able to produce during a trial. Ideally and legally, the discovery should include *all* the information relating to *any* evidence that the D.A. might choose to produce at a trial. However, all this information is not always included and the Defenders sometimes need to request it.)

Based on the file contents, Defenders begin forming an opinion concerning the value of a case.[16] This is illustrated in Karl's comments:

> [W]hen you first open up the case you have [plea bargaining] in mind. When you open up the case and you take a look at the counts, for example, just take a look at the complaint itself. The first time you open up the file folder and take a look at that, you're thinking in terms of 'What is the probable offer I'm gonna get in this case? How much is my client really looking at?' Then you take a look at the bail reduction sheet or the Central Intake report that gives you some sort of inkling as to what the person's prior record is, what their background is, what their age is, sex, racial [inaudible], all those things come into it and you start putting it into your mind as to what you're gonna get as an offer. *Then you read the facts of the case – at least the prosecution's interpretation of what the facts are, through the police reports. And you take a look from that how strong a case they feel they have.* [Emphasis added.]

As Karl states, a critical component of the defendant's case file is the prosecutor's rendition of the facts. From this, the Defenders develop a sense of what story the prosecution could present at court hearings. The Defenders' initial appraisal of this information is a tacit, taken-for-granted assessment which occurs with about as much effort as it takes teachers to grade or evaluate students' research papers: it is not that they tenaciously evaluate every evidentiary ingredient, but instead they note certain 'holes', 'gaps' or 'issues' in the prosecutor's case as they read it.[17]

According to Sudnow (1965), public defenders presume guilt. The only issue in their assessment of cases is whether an alleged crime is 'normal'. 'Normal crimes' are constructs involving concepts of typical offenders who commit certain types of crimes in typical manners, in typical places, and often involve typical victims. These constructs signify to public defenders what offers for guilty pleas their clients will receive.

This study suggests that Sudnow may not have delved deeply enough into public defenders' tacit understandings prior to plea bargaining. Although the Defenders employ normal crime constructs when assessing offers for guilty pleas (discussed further below), they also gauge the strength of evidence in each individual case. Moreover, in assessing evidence, they draw upon knowledge of 'typical weaknesses' in prosecution cases.

Typical weaknesses are deficiencies in prosecution cases that occur with relative frequency. These understandings comprise part of the Defenders' legal expertise and are acquired through their experiences of reading police reports, conducting investigations and taking cases to trial. They include such axioms as 'prosecutors typically overcharge defendants', 'eyewitnesses to crimes frequently have problems identifying offenders', and 'some types of witnesses are reluctant or unable to testify satisfactorily'. Perhaps most important, knowledge of typical weaknesses includes the very keen awareness that police officers routinely embellish or omit information from their reports in order to convict defendants. As three Defenders explained,

> Tom: After a while you get to the point where you read these police reports sort of like the Russians read Pravda. I mean y'know, you read between the lines. You know when they're leaving things out ... The police don't put in their reports the things which are gonna make it impossible for them to convict the defendant.

> Steve: Usually I decide [to write suppression motions] without ever talking to the client ... from having ... read enough police reports and knowing the type of tricks they use to make illegal searches legal, at least on the face of the ... police report.

> Mindy: After reading so many, you kind of see patterns in police reports. You can see whether something is bullshit or whether it's legit. If it's strictly a police bust and it's not a victim complaint, I tend to read it with a real grain of salt.

The Defenders' awareness of typical weaknesses is consequential because it alerts them to possible weaknesses in new cases that otherwise might go undetected. However, while they are significant, it is important to note that they are not the only deficiencies that they spot. Instead, these weaknesses as well as others are all breaches of the Defenders' understanding of evidence as prescribed by their legal community. More specifically, weaknesses in the prosecution case are ascertained along any or all of the interrelated dimensions of sufficiency, legality and persuasiveness. In other words, to be considered strong evidence, the prosecutor must be able to tell a sufficient, legal and persuasive story.

As stated earlier, to be 'sufficient', the prosecution's account must be able to document all the elements of the hypothesis alleged to be true. More precisely, the prosecutor must be able to produce enough information at a trial to suggest that 1) all the elements of a specific crime as defined by the state's penal code occurred, and 2) the defendant committed that crime. He or she must be able to do this for each crime he or she asserts the defendant committed. For example, in response to the question 'What is it you're looking for when reading the case?' Tom explained:

> Whether [the prosecutor] can prove the case ... to find out whether the elements of the crime are there. [For example, the prosecutors and police] will charge someone with a non-divertible 'possession for sale' offense simply because the drugs they have in their possession is of a certain quantity or it's packaged in a certain way [i.e., it is a typical weakness] ... So I look at every one of those cases and I start asking where's the real evidence that this person *sold*? ... Do they have any ledgers? ... [etc.] ... Another thing that you look for is witnesses. Are the victims gonna be people who wanna come to court? [i.e., is it a typical weakness?] Lets say it's a husband beating up his wife. Is she gonna want to come to court? Lets say it's a transient victim ... [etc.] ... Is that guy gonna be around at the time of the preliminary hearing?

If the Defenders postulate that the prosecutor will probably not be able to produce information at a court hearing to document fully all of his or her contentions, they conclude the prosecutor has some weak evidence. They rarely conclude, however, that the prosecutor is unable to document that the defendant committed any crime whatsoever.

To be considered 'legal', any story that the prosecution presents at a trial must fall within the guidelines of those governing laws described earlier. Because these laws are embedded in volumes of case law and statutes, it might seem logical that every time the Defenders receive a new felony case, a flurry of legal research results. In reality, however, legal research does not occur in this manner. Instead, it transpires only after the Defender first spots a potential 'issue'. (The Defenders frequently refer to this as 'issue spotting'.)

The Defenders spot issues for legal research on the basis of their 'legal expertise'. As discussed earlier, this expertise is acquired at law school as well as through their daily practice of law. More precisely, what the Defenders regard as the legal guidelines for evidentiary stories is tacitly and routinely governed by those laws with which they have prior experience. Other laws are overlooked until prosecutors invoke one of them or a Defender updates him or herself in preparation for trial or the filing of a motion.[18] Nora explained how she spots issues for legal research in the following comments:

> You read the case and things jump off the page at you. You say, 'Wait a minute! Wait a minute! I think that's an issue that I want to look into'. ... Or sometimes you're talking to another attorney, and they tell you 'What about this?' 'Have you thought about that?'

In the following excerpts, Vera and Janet describe how weaknesses regarding police arrest procedures (quite possibly typical weaknesses) breached their sense of legal proprieties:

> Vera: I had a case where – my client is Black and he was standing on the street corner in [a poor, predominantly minority section of the city] at 11:00 at night with about ten other guys. And the cop testified that it was dangerous there, and there had been all these shootings there, and these guys were wearing gang colors. So the cops ... got out of their car and lined all these guys up against the wall for their own safety – for the *cops'* safety because they didn't know if they had weapons – patted them down, and found pills ... that was a gap there because these guys were just standing on the street corner – they weren't doing a goddamned thing! ... [Cops] can't just walk up to you and put their hands in your pockets ... [Interviewer: How do you know what the gaps are?] ... [T]here's cases that tell you what has been perceived as 'danger' and what hasn't. You try to think of all the cases that you know.

> Janet: [T]here's a burglary committed and they run after this guy and they lose him. Later on they see him again, and he goes into a house, and they just go right into the house. And there in the house is all the stolen property. Well, the entry into the house was illegal ... because he's not a fleeing felon anymore. They just saw him two days later and they just burst into the house. *And you know it's absolutely wrong* ... They could have got a warrant. [Emphasis added]

For the Defender to conclude that the prosecutor's rendition of facts is legal, it must fall within the guidelines of those previously researched and cited laws that constitute his or her tacit repertoire for understanding legal procedure and the admissibility of evidence. If any part does not, it transgresses the Defender's sense of prevailing legal protocol. He or she then considers that information either blatantly inadmissible or (more likely) a weak spot and possible point of dispute during a court hearing.

To be 'persuasive', any story that the prosecution presents must be able to construct a credible account of the defendant's alleged crime. The Defenders gauge the persuasiveness of stories by scrutinizing their congruity (or incongruity) with what they assume is the judge and jury's commonsense awareness.[19] This is illustrated in Janet's elaboration on how she evaluated one case against a defendant:

> [T]he police report [said] 'I saw this guy walking down the street and he did something which caused me to contact him'. All right? 'So I contacted him and decided to pat him down for weapons. And I felt a bulky object, and I pulled it out, and it was a baggie of marijuana'. Right there I know that a baggie of marijuana doesn't feel like a weapon [i.e., it breached her common sense]. *So there you know you have an issue on the pat-down.* [Emphasis added.]

Steve's comments reveal not merely his own commonsense assumption that there is only one objective and intersubjective world (Pollner, 1974), but also his conviction that the judge and jury will find contradictions to this assumption (i.e., two accounts of symptoms which indicate two divergent realities regarding drug use) implausible:

> [In examining the prosecutor's case,] I look at the symptomology [sic] [of alleged drug use] that the police officers mark on their police report *to see if it's consistent with their lab's analysis ... If I saw a contradictory symptomology ... then I do a retest.* [Emphasis added]

When any part of the prosecutor's story appears inconsonant with common sense, it breaches the Defender's sense of prevailing social conventions and is considered a weak spot. On the other hand, when no such weaknesses are apparent and the information is situated favorably within the traditional social hierarchy and structure of authority, it is deemed extremely believable and difficult, if not impossible, to impeach.[20] Lacking any obvious inconsistencies in law enforcement narratives, for example, Steve does not question the credibility of crime lab results. Yet publicity throughout the mid and late 1990s concerning the behavior of law enforcement in the O.J. Simpson murder case and the F.B.I. crime lab make it clear that such scientific reports are subject to error if not outright falsehoods. Instead, Steve merely deems such information extremely tenable. Similarly, Ingmar explains that, despite his own mistrust of police officers:

> [Like judges, a] jury doesn't want to believe that a police officer can lie either. A police officer is like Dick Tracy. Perfect. Always with the right motives, and very well trained, and all that.

In sum, upon reviewing the story that the prosecution could present at court hearings, Defenders tacitly evaluate it along the dimensions of sufficiency, legality and persuasiveness. If the story seems adequate along these three dimensions, it is tentatively viewed as a strong case. Otherwise, it is considered to have one or more weaknesses. No final conclusion is reached, however, until the Defender considers how he or she might respond to the prosecutor's allegations.

Building and Assessing a Possible Defense Case

Legally, defense attorneys are not responsible for proving a defendant's innocence. Rather, it is the prosecutor's obligation to prove guilt. However, Defenders maintain that in order to win a case, they must cast 'reasonable doubt', or, elicit information during a court hearing that counters prosecution claims. Consequently, after their initial appraisal of the prosecutor's case, they consider how they might respond with an alternative narrative.

To be viable, a defense story must enable the Defender to convince a judge or jury that the prosecution story is insufficient, illegal and/or reasonably uncertain if not completely unbelievable. At the same time, the defense story must itself be sufficient, legal and persuasive. Otherwise, they believe judging authorities will find their own account deficient.

There are two important sources from which Defenders attempt to draw information to build a defense story. These are the prosecution case and the defendant.

The Prosecution Case as Source The Defenders view any weakness in the prosecution case as a possible defense. Thus, while they search for 'holes', 'gaps' or 'issues' in the prosecution case, they are at the same time searching for viable defenses. This is illustrated in Tom's précis:

> I had a case dismissed earlier this year where the police got a report that a man was being attacked by some other people. And they went to the scene and the people who had been doing the attacking were gone. And the man who had been attacked reportedly ran into a bar. And [the police went into the bar] and asked 'Are you the guy who was being attacked?' and '[Do you need] any help?' And the guy said, 'No, I wasn't. And I don't need any help'. And the police proceeded to leave, but on the way out one of the patrons in the bar said 'That's the guy that they were chasing'. So they went back and said, 'Why did you lie to us?' and then patted him down ... [I]nside each one of the matchbooks [they found on him] was a little sliver of methamphetamine ... *It was clear on reading the police report that ... they didn't have any real criteria to suggest that he was anything but the victim of other people.* [Emphasis added]

In this incident, Tom foresaw that, framed within his own argument, a police officer's account could breach the judge's commonsense and legal sensibilities of acceptable evidentiary stories: because the judge should realize that victims, by definition, are not miscreants, he or she should realize the police officer did not have any commonsense or legal right to detain and search the defendant. Thus, he (correctly) anticipated he could elicit information during a court hearing (or construct a defense story) that would render the prosecution evidence (or story) unpersuasive, illegal and therefore insufficient.

Similarly, William recounted how a weakness in another prosecution case signaled a potential defense:

> I recently had a case that involved robbery of a lady who was putting gasoline in her truck in broad daylight. Robber hit her in the head, took the contents of her purse, started walking down the street, she screamed, 'Help!' Two Hispanic individuals followed him in their vehicle ... he pulled a gun ... [and they left] ... [T]he defendant was not picked-up on that day but three days later when the victim saw him on a

street-corner. So, those kind of facts scream out for an
identification type issue.

In this instance, William spotted a typical weakness in prosecution cases that
could spell a violation of common sense. Based on his commonsense
understanding that people who are actually acquainted with another are
typically able to recognize that person, as well as his understanding that crime
victims frequently encounter problems identifying strange and fleeting
aggressors, he speculated he might be able to develop a legal, sufficient and
persuasive defense narrative that would render the prosecution story
implausible to a jury.

When Defenders perceive a weakness in the prosecution case (or
conversely, a conceivable defense), some type of research or investigation
typically occurs to determine whether a viable defense story might *actually* be
constructed. In the robbery case described above, for example, William
continued to state:

> So the thought crossed my mind of possibly a line-up ... to
> determine whether or not these people would be able to
> identify my client. In that case what I did was I put together
> a line-up of photos – none of which contained my client. I
> wanted to see exactly how good these peoples' perceptions
> [were]. Sure enough, they all picked out people who were not
> my client. And I figured that's gonna help my case. That's
> what I mean by seeing the issue and then trying to undermine
> the D.A.

Likewise, Ingmar explained that

> Sometimes you just notice the issues and you don't know the
> answer all the time. And then you do research and find out.
> Spotting the issues is one thing, and, I mean, you always have
> to do some research on it.

The Defendant as Source Upon interviewing defendants, Defenders look for
viable rebuttals to alleged criminal incidents. Tom, for example, explained that
his interviews with clients consist of

> Talking about the case. [Interviewer: What about?] 'Tell me
> about the case'. I'll have read the discovery [and] I'll ask

them questions about the things that are important to making
the case. I'll say, 'Well they said "this." Is this true? ... Were
you there? Did you do this?'

Ingmar explains how he seeks accounts from defendants that might render
illegal the prosecution story:

You ask [yourself while reading the police report] 'Did the
cops do anything illegal?' And when your client's telling you
what the cops did ... you always ask your client 'Is that how
it happened?' Or, 'How did it happen?'

Ingmar's and Steve's comments reveal, however, that defendants sometimes
provide accounts that do not conform to legal recipes for viable defense
stories:

[I]f there's nothing to suppress [i.e., statements or physical
evidence], you don't have a motion to suppress [the
evidence]. A lot of people say, 'Well, they didn't give me my
rights'. ... [And I respond,] 'Well, did you make any
incriminating statements to them? ... Did they find
anything?' [And they state,] 'No'. [And I respond,] 'Well,
too bad ... You can sue them ... but ... you have to have
something to suppress [to file a suppression motion]'.

[S]ometimes the defendant gives you an account which
equates to being guilty of the charge [legally] even though
they thought they were right ... I guess battery cases [are
good examples] because most clients think that if they didn't
punch somebody at least that it's not a battery, where in fact
the law states that any harmful or offensive touching
[constitutes battery].

Mindy's comments show how Defenders examine accounts for defenses that
may portray the prosecution story as *insufficient*:

[I]f your intention is something other than robbery, you may
have some other crime there, but you don't have 'kidnap for
robbery' ... [T]he story that came out [in one case] was that
my client and his friend forced this prostitute into a motel

room, and their intent was to get her off the street so they could privately talk to her about working for them. They were pimps ... [A]nd when they weren't able to convince her ... he asked her if she had any money. And she said 'No', and his friend searched her and found some money. *And so if you determine that the thought of the robbery came later, and that the purpose in taking her to the motel room was to discuss this business negotiation, then that's not a kidnap for robbery.* [Emphasis added]

While Mindy's remarks indicate that viable defense stories are able to render prosecution stories insufficient, they also reveal her recognition that the *best* defense stories should render prosecution claims *completely* insufficient. Otherwise, they are themselves not wholly sufficient. The defendant might not be guilty of 'kidnap for robbery', for example, but he might be found guilty of some other crime.

Robert insists that a good defense story must be 'persuasive', or, one that is consistent with a judging authority's common sense:

[B]y and large you have to be able to rationally and consistently and reasonably respond to the allegations. You gotta do it for reasonable people sitting in the jury box.

In the following excerpt, Janet describes how a typical weakness in one prosecution case developed into a potentially persuasive defense story upon interviewing a witness:

I just had a case where I didn't think there was a big issue but [the police report] said, 'He had a tail light out, so I pulled him over. He had a marijuana joint behind his ear and there was a baggie of rock cocaine just sitting there on the console in between the seats'. It sounds like a lie. It turns out that the girlfriend, when I talked to her, [stated] ... she had just fixed the tail lights. So I knew they were lying about that.

In this incident, common sense dictated to Janet that new or newly repaired items do not typically malfunction. She therefore envisioned that, perhaps with further documentation of a fixed tail light, a judge might find a police officer's testimony implausible and therefore the prosecution story as illegal and insufficient to convict the defendant.

It is critical to note here that Janet began her commentary by stating that, despite her suspicion that the police officer was lying, she originally 'didn't think there was a big issue'. Those remarks were based on her unspoken understanding that even though she knows police officers routinely lie, judging authorities do not. Instead, these court actors are expected to believe that a person stopped by a police officer was stupid enough to display illegal drugs openly rather than to believe a police officer lied. Without supplementary information, Janet assumed the latter was too inconsistent with the judge and jury's conventional value and belief system (or, common sense) to be believable.

Nora describes a case in which she believed the jury would find a defense story unpersuasive due not simply to the defendant's status but her lower class lifestyle. In this instance, Nora expected that certain facts about the defendant's lifestyle would enter into a court hearing and be so divergent from mainstream values, beliefs and norms that the jury would find the account implausible:

> I have a client who is a prostitute. And a transvestite [friend] came by and asked her ... 'Could you drive my car [and meet me] somewhere?' And my client did ... and got stopped by the police for having no license plate. And [the car turned out to be] stolen and [my client] had no idea. And the jury is really not going to relate too well to transvestites and prostitutes. That's pretty far removed from where they are. I guess they're also pretty far removed from having friends who would put them in that kind of situation. Their lives are a lot more orderly, safe than people like my client.

William explains that although evidentiary stories benefit from ingredients that are favorably situated within the jury's commonsense value and belief system, Defenders represent clients who are typically unable to provide such ingredients:

> If you look at a case like DeLorian [a car manufacturer acquitted of money laundering] – that case, somebody very wealthy, he had an excellent appearance ... I think that affected the jury's impression of him. Whereas our clients usually are not [employed], haven't been for awhile, don't have much education, they don't look real good ... so that does have an effect on the jury's [thinking].

If the Defender concludes after interviewing a defendant that there might be a viable defense story with which to counter prosecution claims, she engages in some legal research or begins an investigation. Otherwise, she concludes there is nothing to research or investigate.

Weighing the Evidence: The Scales of Justice in Action

Defenders conclude their imaginary courtroom dialogue by mentally 'weighing' the colloquy on a conceptual scales of justice: on one side of the scales is placed the prosecution story, and on the other side is placed the defense story. The more the defense story is able to counterweight (or offset) the prosecutor's, the stronger the defense case is believed to be. Conversely, the less it is able to counterweight (or offset) the prosecution story, the stronger prosecution evidence is believed to be.

Mather (1979) found that defense attorneys classify cases into three categories that have definite implications regarding the decision to plea bargain. The results of Defenders' weighing activity can be characterized similarly. The possible outcomes range along a continuum. At one end of the continuum fall 'reasonable doubt' cases. At the other end are 'dead bang losers'. In between the two extremes are cases best identified as 'overfiled reasonable doubt'.

'Reasonable doubt' cases are those the Defenders believe can be won or dismissed because a story equivalent to or better than the prosecution's can be presented.[21] For example, in one case being prepared for trial, the defendant was accused of stealing more than $15,000 worth of jewelry from a home and then pawning the stolen property. The prosecutor maintained the defendant was guilty not only because witnesses stated he had attended the party that took place at the victim's house at the time of the theft, but also because several pawn store employees provided descriptions of the suspect that closely resembled the defendant.

The defendant, however, stated that another man, who also attended the party and who looked remarkably similar to him, was the actual culprit. In addition, the defendant could furnish a picture of the 'real' thief as well as a witness besides himself (i.e., his employer) who would testify that the defendant was working at the time of the pawn store exchange.

In this case, the Defender concluded she could summon information during a trial that was at least equally as legal, sufficient and persuasive as the prosecutor's: the two defense witnesses along with the unspoken 'testimony' of the picture were comparable to the prosecutor's witnesses. Thus, the defense case counterweighted or offset completely the prosecution case.

In another 'reasonable doubt' case, the defendant was charged with 'driving under the influence with injury' and 'child endangerment'. The police report stated that the defendant was involved in an accident in which one of his children was hurt. His blood alcohol level was found to be .11.

The Defender believed this case was triable for several reasons. First, the defendant insisted the accident was due not to intoxication but instead to a diversion 'by something that anyone could have been distracted by'. Second, the defendant and his children all stated they had their seat belts on. Third, the client was very articulate and would have made a very good witness.[22] Finally, the Defender had located an expert witness who would testify that while the defendant was driving, his alcohol level could have been within the legal limit of .10.

Like the previously cited Defender, this one believed she could match the prosecution story with an equivalent defense story: she anticipated she could communicate comparably legal, sufficient and persuasive information to intimate that her client was *not* involved in an accident due to intoxication and that he did *not* endanger his children.

It is important to mention here that evidence presented on behalf of defendants in these cases would not have proven their innocence: it is quite *possible* that they actually committed the crimes. Instead, the information presented would have been enough *simply to counterweight or offset* the prosecutor's evidence.

'Dead bang losers' are cases that the Defenders conclude cannot be won because the defense story does not at all offset the prosecutor's. A case which illustrates this category is one in which the defendant was charged with three counts of burglary. According to the police report, the defendant had assisted another man with the purchase of goods from three different stores with stolen credit cards. He told the police that another man had given him the cards to throw away, but instead of complying, he gave the cards to a friend who then began buying goods. The defendant later changed his story, however, and told the police that he did not know the cards were stolen or that his friend's name was not on the cards.

According to the Defender, his client was in 'big trouble' for several reasons. First, the defendant had admitted to knowing the credit cards were stolen. Second, his friend stated the defendant was involved with prior knowledge. Lastly, other witnesses could testify to his behavior in the stores.

In this case, the Defender could have produced legal and sufficient information at a trial to counter prosecution claims. For example, the defendant could have adhered to his second story and insisted that his friend was mistaken and that the police officers were lying. However, even though

Defenders contend they routinely lie, police officers are deemed extremely credible. Thus, the defense story was not considered *persuasive* enough to offset the prosecutor's.

Another 'dead bang loser' case was one in which a 'stubborn' defendant insisted on taking his case to trial. The defendant had been charged with burglary. The prosecutor had two witnesses, a mother and daughter who were neighbors to the victim. The mother stated she had been asked by the victim's conservator to 'keep an eye on the house'.

Both prosecution witnesses stated they saw the defendant standing outside their apartment with another suspect, who was actually holding the stolen TV. They said they followed the defendant down an alley and when they were spotted, both the defendant and the other suspect hurriedly walked away. In addition, the mother insisted she was familiar with the defendant and 'would know him anywhere'.

On the other hand, the defendant stated he was watching TV with his mother and girlfriend during the alleged burglary. He also claimed that while the prosecution witnesses stated his hair was in braids, his hair was not braided at the time of the burglary.

Although the defendant provided an alternative account of the alleged criminal incident, upon investigating the issues and comparing the two cases, the Defender did not believe he could adequately counter the prosecution story. He reached his conclusion for four reasons. First, having interviewed the defendant's mother, he believed she would make a poor witness because she easily lost her temper and would probably lose it in front of a jury upon questioning by the prosecutor. Second, the defendant was deemed unable to testify on his own behalf because of a burglary record.[23] Third, the prosecution witnesses had no 'obvious' (or 'commonsense') motive to lie while the defense witnesses did.[24] And finally, one prosecution witness – the mother – was very articulate and would make a good impression on the jury. Thus, while the defendant in this case could produce legal and sufficient information at a trial, the story was deemed not *persuasive* enough to counterweight the prosecutor's.

It is important to interject here that the prosecution's 'strong' evidence in these cases did not necessarily mean the defendants were guilty: it is quite *possible* that both defendants were actually innocent. Instead, the defense stories were considered completely unable *to counterweight or offset* any of the prosecution story.

'Overfiled reasonable doubt' cases are those which the Defenders believe could offset *some* but not all of the prosecution story. In the burglary case described above, for example, the Defender believed the defendant would have been better off pleading guilty to the less serious charge of 'aiding and abetting'. This was because, although prosecution witnesses could imply the defendant presented a guilty appearance by running away (a fact the Defender foresaw as irrefutable), they could not actually state that they saw the defendant inside the burglarized house or even holding the stolen goods. Consequently, the Defender envisioned he could elicit legal, sufficient and persuasive information from the prosecution's own witnesses to offset the hypothesis that the defendant committed 'burglary' (i.e., 'illegal *entry* with *the intent to commit* theft or some felony') but not 'aiding and abetting' a felon.

To allay confusion about how the same case could possibly fall into two different categories, it should be emphasized here that the two sets of circumstances would have entailed dissimilar stories. In the first situation, the defendant completely denied any involvement whatsoever in the incident. Thus, the Defender maintained that the jury would be forced to decide whose account of the alleged burglary was more believable. He concluded that they were likely to believe the prosecution. In the second situation, the defendant would have to admit that he was at the scene. The jury might then be able to find him guilty of the less serious charge.

Another 'overfiled reasonable doubt' case involved a man charged with four counts of molesting his stepdaughter. The complaining witness stated that the defendant once forced her into oral copulation, twice forced her into anal and vaginal intercourse, and improperly touched her at one other time. A medical report produced findings consistent with child molestation (i.e., some stretch marks in the vaginal area).

The Defender had accepted this case from another attorney and she claimed she would have settled it if the defendant had been 'reasonable'. However, the case was going to trial and the Defender hoped to show bias and fabrication on the part of the complaining witness, not because the child's intent was to 'get' her stepfather, but because her mother put her up to it: upon investigating the matter, the Defender discovered that prior to disclosure of the allegations, the mother had asked a male acquaintance what it would take for the two to get together. Among other things, the male acquaintance stated that her husband would have to be 'out of the picture'. Three days later, the mother told a friend of the family that her husband had been molesting her daughter. The friend asked the child if this was true and she said 'Yes'. The mother and friend then contacted another friend, called 'Chicken Leg', who talked to the child. The child did not provide Chicken Leg with detailed narratives of what happened but instead responded to his descriptions. The police were called the next day. After the child was removed from the home, the mother began dating the first male acquaintance.

The Defender also intended to bring in her own expert witness to evaluate the prosecutor's medical evidence. This expert was going to state that the physical evidence was not consistent with the child's claims (i.e., the child had an intact hymen and there was no evidence of force) but instead that it was compatible with a realm of other possibilities.

In her rebuttal, the Defender planned on using a doctor and two friends of the family as witnesses. Because the defendant had a prior conviction of child molestation, she was uncertain whether she would use his testimony. If she decided to do so, she stated it would enter the trial only as an unspecified prior conviction (i.e., it would be 'sanitized').

On the surface, this case might appear to be a good triable case: because it was not essential that the defendant testify, it might seem the Defender was able to capitulate a commensurate legal, sufficient and persuasive account that the defendant did not molest his stepdaughter but instead was framed by his wife. However, because their lifestyles diverged from middle-class standards, she worried that her witnesses might not be as persuasive as the victim given community sentiment regarding children generally and child molestation in particular. Thus, she deemed the defense unable to counterweight fully the prosecution story and despaired that the defendant would lose the case and suffer serious legal sanctions because he would not plead to the less disputable and less serious charge of 'improper touching'.

Evaluating the Defendant's Background

In interviewing their clients, Defenders also solicit additional information regarding their backgrounds. As Robert explained,

> [Interviewer: What do you talk to the defendant about?] His case. [Interviewer: What about?] ... [I] ask him for generally his individual background information. [Interviewer: Such as?] Where he lives, who he lives with, how old he is, his date of birth, how long he's been living wherever he is, and where's he from. Whether – not necessarily all in this order – whether he has any drug or alcohol problems, whether he's married and has children, is employed, where he's been employed before, whether his family is here in town or elsewhere, where they are, what family is around and available and that he has contact with. Has he ever been in a mental hospital, does he have any serious medical problems?

Did he serve in the military, does he have any prior convictions and what were they. Did he serve in the penitentiary or just jail for those offenses? And then I usually try and go over the police reports with him. [Interviewer: Before the police reports, what is the purpose of asking him all those questions?] ... [I]t may all have a lot of relevance [to his case]. Family situation may ultimately have something to do with the case, or at sentencing, you may want to show the support of family, or try to show the support of family. If he has any psychiatric background, I want to know about it. It may have relevance to the case ... [I]t may have relevance to trial, or it may have relevance at sentencing.

As suggested in Robert's comments as well as earlier discussions, Defenders expect information about defendants' social backgrounds to effectuate images among judges and jurors of not simply 'who' they are but moreover whether they are (in essence) moral risks or 'hazards'.[25] In gauging case values, Defenders elicit this information to determine how agreeable, reputable and/or commendable they will be to judging authorities. In general, the more a client's background (including his or her prior offense record) can be seen to conform with traditional commonsense standards, the more respect they are expected to evoke. This is illustrated in the following comments:

Robert: Members of the underclass have – it is a subculture in which certain things are accepted, or tolerated which may not be tolerated by jurors who come from more of a mainstream kind of background. Living together with girlfriends, children out of wedlock, situations like that which may not be as well-accepted by jurors, those kinds of factors play heavily ... [I]f you're able to present to the jury a defendant who is a working stiff, that makes him a much more loveable kind of person, a sympathetic kind of person, a person more like the jurors, and is a great advantage. And if the defendant is truly indigent, that's not something you can do for him.

William: [In interviewing defendants,] I'm naturally testing their credibility to some extent. Just by listening to what they have to say, evaluating what kind of witness they'll be ... [Interviewer: Do you look at priors?] Yes. That's one thing

I neglected to mention. In assessing what kind of witness they're gonna be and what kind of problems you're gonna have in a case ... if he or she has priors, we're absolutely gonna have to discuss those ... [Interviewer: Do priors come in any other way?] If you mean do they make me think that this person is more likely to have done it, not really. You know, it depends on how close the facts are I suppose. *More in terms of what kind of witness they will be and how the jurors will assess their credibility if they have priors.* [Emphasis added.]

Estimating the Cost of Plea Bargaining

After evaluating the strength of evidence and the defendant's social background, Defenders compare the cost likely to be incurred upon plea bargaining to that of taking the case to trial. These cost comparisons are made by drawing upon understandings of what Sudnow (1965) has called 'normal crimes'.

Sudnow found that Public Defenders' concepts of 'normal crimes' (i.e., crimes which are committed in typical manners in typical places and which involve typical offenders and victims) signify to them what offers for guilty pleas their clients will receive.[26] Similarly, Defenders expect a 'typical' crime to be reduced in a 'typical' manner. However, when the criminal case is atypical in some manner (i.e., the crime is more or less serious than usual, the evidence is unusually strong or weak, and/or the defendant is more or less respectable than average), they expect a commensurate atypical reduction of some sort. These principles are illustrated in the following accounts:

Tom [He is discussing what a 'reasonable' offer for a guilty plea is.]*: Your standard offer* on a felony is probation and a guarantee of local time. And so, assume you've got a client with a Class III felony charge. In most instances what's gonna happen is you're gonna go to the dispo department and the D.A.'s gonna offer you a felony NOLT – which means 'not opposed to local time', probation. Now, *if the client has no record at all and it's not a particularly serious offense, or if there's some big 4th Amendment problem which even the prosecution recognizes*, then the offer may come down. It may come down to a misdemeanor. It may come down to a misdemeanor in twelve months. It may come down to immediate sentencing and credit for time served. It may come down to a lot of things ... On the other hand, *if the person's got a heavier record*, then they may not be offered a NOLT, they may be offered a mid-term lid. Or if it's a complicated case, they may be offered 'plead to one count, dismiss the remaining counts, sentenced to court' – in which case the person may be looking at prison. [Emphasis added]

Steve: [Interviewer: How do you decide whether it's a good or bad offer?] Well, based on two things. What their standard offer is – which on a battery is a $300 fine and plead to the charge – and how severe the facts are in the case, or how weak they are. *If it's an average case, then I consider it an average offer.* And whether they've never been arrested before, or whether they have a long arrest record. That's assuming a one count complaint. Usually – or at least half the time, there would be a second count. Battery. Vandalism. Spousal Battery. [Interviewer: How do you know what the standard offer is?] From experience. If you don't know, you go ask somebody who's done more of those cases. [Emphasis added.]

Thus, for a 'normal' or average crime, the Defenders expect the typical, average or standard offer. In other words, the value of the case is average. For an atypical case, which means that the alleged crime, the defendant, and/or the strength of the evidence is better or worse than average, they expect commensurately greater or less incentive for their client to plead guilty. In other words, the case is commensurately more or less valuable than average.

Upon discerning the value of a case, the Defenders compare the penalties associated with plea bargaining to that of taking the case to trial. Cases with great value are generally thought to be associated with little cost for pleading guilty and, depending on their client's preference in light of other personal circumstances,[27] the Defenders are apt to conclude that these defendants will be better off by accepting a plea bargain. On the other hand, Defenders are likely to encourage clients whose cases have little value to go to trial. This is because these defendants are thought to have little or nothing to lose by doing so. Ironically, this means that Defenders are more likely to encourage those defendants charged with more serious crimes, who have lengthier prior records, and against whom the prosecutor has stronger evidence to take their cases to trial.[28]

Conclusion

In determining the value of a case, Defenders develop a professional opinion as to the potential benefits and drawbacks of settling it. This information then comprises the crux of their subsequent counsel to clients. Precisely how they counsel clients about their options as well as negotiate the terms of plea bargains will be discussed in Chapter Five. At this point, however, it is important to consider whether the manner in which they develop their opinions entails justice for the poor.

Contrary to the popular image of publicly provided attorneys, Defenders do not presume their clients' guilt or assume that their cases should be plea bargained. Instead, they gauge the strength of evidence (and thereby the probability of conviction for a crime through trial) and then compare the likely sentences after a trial and through plea bargaining. When they believe their clients have little or nothing to lose by taking their cases to trial, they recommend trial. On the other hand, when the cost of a guilty plea seems minimal, their professional opinion at least implicitly suggests that case settlement may be best. Overall then, in assessing case values, protecting the client's interest is the fundamental concern, and the Defender's loyalty should be seen to rest *not* with D.A.s and judges, but instead with defendants.

Nonetheless, some observers might find fault with the Defender's behavior on two counts. First, evidentiary considerations might not be as scrupulous as some might desire. Rather than taking a more aggressive, proactive stance toward research and investigation, for example, Defenders assume a more passive, reactive posture. Thus, they may be less likely to find viable defense stories than attorneys who represent wealthy clients with greater access to resources. Yet it is important to realize that this does not entail discrimination solely against the poor but also involves working-class and middle-class persons who also have less access to resources than the wealthy.

Second, it might be argued that while defendants should legally be found guilty beyond *any* reasonable doubt, Defenders postulate that only defense rhetoric that is equally *or more* plausible than the prosecution's will acquit their clients. This rather subtly shifts the burden of proof from the prosecution to the defense, and implies that the rights of at least some of their clients may be abridged. Infringements are especially likely in cases where defense allies are not situated comparably with prosecution witnesses among status quo sentiments; i.e., the poorest of the poor are most apt to suffer.

Yet assuming the Defenders' calculations accurately reflect adjudicators' reality, one might counter this argument by stating that this behavior is actually ethical because it limits unwarranted costs and thereby brings about greater equity than would otherwise be obtained. This brings us to an alternative manner by which social class influences assessments of cases for plea bargaining. Specifically, although some might argue that the Defenders are not performing altogether optimally, the greatest injustice for the poor infiltrates assessments of cases through the relationship these attorneys envision between poor defendants and judging authorities. Namely, because poor defendants are unable to emulate status quo standards of respectability, they are less likely to have commendable social backgrounds and more likely to have unconvincing defense rhetoric (or 'weak evidence'). Ironically, this does *not* mean they are more likely to plea bargain. It *does* mean, however, that they are more likely to be convicted of crimes and, by implication, more likely to have higher rates of conviction, more serious prior offense records and more severe sentences *regardless of* their actual innocence or guilt.[29]

Notes

1 E.g., Guggenheim (1986), Lerner (1986), and Nelson (1988).
2 E.g., Blumberg (1967a and b), Eisenstein and Jacob (1977), and Sudnow (1965).
3 E.g., Alschuler (1975; 1986), and Blumberg (1967b).
4 E.g., Platt and Pollock (1974).
5 E.g., Farrell (1971), and Swigert and Farrell (1977).
6 E.g., Emmelman (1996), Heumann (1975), Holmes, Daudistel and Farrell (1987), Mather (1979), Maynard (1984a; 1988), McDonald (1985), Neubauer (1974), Rosett and Cressey (1976).
7 Emerson and Paley (1992) have found that prosecutors' concern with convictability results in a 'downstream orientation' or an anticipation of how other court actors will interpret and respond to a case. (See also Frohmann 1991; 1997.) Except that they are concerned with *avoiding* convictions (i.e., protecting their clients' interest) instead of securing them, the Defenders behave similarly.
8 This is consistent with the findings of Eisenstein and Jacob (1977), Feeley (1977), Heuman (1975), Mather (1979), Maynard (1984a), McDonald (1985), Neubauer (1974), Rosett and Cressey (1976) and Utz (1978).
9 See also, Cloyd (1975) and Maroules (1986).
10 C.f., Ewick and Silbey (1995).
11 The police officers' apparently careful documentation of such legalities also indicates their own awareness of laws governing search and seizure, arrest and the admissibility of evidence. For a discussion on how police officers are, in fact, trained to follow legal prescriptions, see Cloyd (1975).
12 See for examples, Black (1993), Brannigan and Lynch (1987), Cooney (1994), Frohmann (1991; 1997), Holmes et al (1987), Homant and Kennedy (1985) Kalven and Zeisel (1976), LaFree (1985a), Lizotte (1978), Matoesian (1995), Maynard (1982; 1984a; 1988), O'Barr (1982), Rabinowitz (1985), Radelet and Pierce (1985), Sanders (1985), Skolnick (1967), Stanko (1982), Swigert and Farrell (1977) and Wiseman (1979).

13 Similarly, Stanko (1982), citing herself as well as Hall (1975), Miller (1970) and Myers and Hagan (1979) states, 'when evidentiary strength is held constant, higher-status victims are likely to increase the prosecutability of a case (:231)'. In addition, Stanko finds that prosecutors employ stereotypical imagery often based on commonsense understandings to assess victim credibility before a jury. (For additional discussions on how actors employ and construct cultural images and stereotypes in other contexts both in and out of court, see Frohmann, 1991; Holstein, 1993; Loeske, 1992; Matoesian, 1995; and Maynard, 1984a.) While Stanko's findings are largely consistent with those reported here, it is important to mention a key distinction: Stanko conceives of evidence in a manner different from that portrayed in this study. She distinguishes between legal sufficiency (or evidentiary strength) and persuasiveness. This study indicates that these two factors are *both* important dimensions of 1) the very concept of evidence itself and 2) evidentiary strength. This means that victim credibility – which includes considerations of their social characteristics, lifestyle, and/or status – should not be considered an extralegal factor but instead as an important dimension of evidence and evidentiary strength. This is discussed further in footnote fifteen below.

14 C.f., Frohmann, 1997.

15 In his analysis of the Kennedy Smith rape trial, Matoesian (1995) argues that the distinction between legal and extralegal factors collapses when examining the language of evidence in testimony (see for example, Reskin and Visher 1986); i.e., through courtroom dialogue, attorneys are able to activate traditional stereotypes about the nature of male/female sexual relations as well as inconsistencies in victim behavior and background. Courtroom dialogue is therefore moral dialogue that defies regulation by rape shield laws.

The findings presented here are consistent with Matoesian's. However, this study further suggests that moral dialogue – including that regarding the social characteristics or backgrounds of witnesses – is inherent in the *very concept* of evidence. To iterate, evidence is persuasive; i.e., it is symbolic and conveys meaning. Persuasiveness (or meaning) is fundamentally ascertained within the cultural framework of common sense. Thus, evidence is both verbal and nonverbal 'testimony' understood from the viewpoint (or with the value and belief system) of the status quo. Evaluations of the social characteristics and backgrounds of 'witnesses' (both animate and inanimate) are therefore integral in evidentiary considerations.

It is also important to reiterate here that, as LaFree's (1985b) findings on Hispanic defendants suggests, it is import to consider the varying cultural contexts of common sense. Common sense should be seen as the values, beliefs and norms of the status quo and since the status quo varies somewhat from place to place, so will the specific values, beliefs and norms used to judge and sentence defendants.

16 At this point, Defenders may also see that the defendant allegedly confessed to the police. Although this will *not* indicate that their client has no defense whatsoever, it does tend to suggest that she is guilty in some capacity and should not expect complete exoneration.

17 Interestingly, in discussing prosecutors' 'downstream concerns' in case assessment, Frohmann suggests that these court actors 'are actively looking for 'holes' or problems that will make the victim's version of 'what happened' unbelievable or not convincing beyond a reasonable doubt (1991: 214).' Together with the findings presented here, this suggests not only that prosecuting and defense attorneys have similar concerns and understandings regarding evidentiary strength, but also that prosecutors are accurately predicting defense attorneys' responses to their cases.

18 It is important to point out here that because the Defenders discuss their cases among themselves, an update on part of one Defender also means the others are updated.

19 This is what Neubauer (1974) appears to mean when he states that both prosecuting and defense attorneys employ 'standards of proof assumed to be maintained by juries' while negotiating plea bargains. Neubauer, however, did not elaborate on the specific character of these standards.

It is also important to note that Stanko (1982) and Frohmann (1991) find that prosecutors screen cases based on commonsense evaluations of how juries will assess the victim. Stanko's findings were described in an earlier footnote. Frohmann finds that prosecutors screen rape cases in part through commonsense assumptions regarding normal heterosexual relations: when victims' post-rape behavior fails to conform with these assumptions, prosecutors deem the victims noncredible. She also finds that prosecutors assess victims' credibility by drawing upon commonsense knowledge regarding comportment.

20 C.f., Cooney (1994), Stanko (1982) and Frohmann (1991).

21 Also included in this category of cases are those that are dismissed because the Defender successfully argues that the police engaged in illegal search and seizure procedures. In these cases, the Defender can be seen to cast reasonable doubt insofar as the prosecutor no longer has sufficient evidence to prove his or her case.

22 This pattern of talk appears to correspond to what O'Barr (1982) has called 'narrativeness.'

23 It is also relevant to point out here that the judge in this case told the Defender 'any defense attorney who let this client testify on his own behalf should be sued for malpractice.' This supports the idea that the other members of their legal community shared many of the Defenders' taken-for-granted understandings regarding the strength of evidence.

24 This is one way in which Black's (in Cooney, 1994) concept of 'social distance' enters into the Defender's consciousness through common sense.

25 The concept of 'moral hazard' derives from Glenn (2000).

26 See also the findings of Mather (1979) and Neubauer (1974).

27 Feeley (1979) has found that because defendants in a lower criminal court are apt to incur a relatively large number of pre-trial costs (such as lost wages, attorney retainer fees, jail time, and bail money), they are more apt to plea bargain. Although the Defenders do not themselves consider these factors in their assessment of case values, these costs do tend to be issues for some defendants who express their concerns and preferences to their attorneys. Some of these defendants, however, find the cost of pleading guilty to outweigh the cost of going to trial.

28 This is supported by Harris and Springer's (1984) finding that attorneys who represent clients with serious prior records will be more likely to go to trial than to plea bargain. Their finding may reflect the fact that prosecutors offer defendants whose cases have little value only little incentive to plea bargain. Consequently, these defendants have little or nothing to lose by taking their case to trial.

29 This study indicates that social class influences adjudication outcomes not only as an extra-legal variable *but also as a component of legal variables*. More will be said about this in the conclusion to this book.

Chapter Four

Taking Cases to Trial

For most people, jury trial epitomizes the adversarial ideal: it is through jury trial that criminal cases are thoroughly investigated, the validity of certain laws and legal procedures are thoroughly tested-out, and the defendant's legal guilt is thoroughly litigated. Despite this perception, jury trial is the least frequent mode of case disposal. In addition, publicly provided defense attorneys are commonly believed to provide their clients with the least rigorous services throughout this ordeal.[1] This chapter examines how Defenders litigate their client's guilt of crime through jury trials.

The decision to take a case to trial results in two types of activities. These are case preparation and the conduct of formal proceedings. These activities are discussed below.

Preparing the Defense Case: Constructing a Viable Defense Story

For the most part, the Defenders' preparation of a case for trial is a constant, cumulative, and progressive type of activity: they usually begin preparing immediately upon deciding to take the case to trial and then continue to engage in some type of preparation until a verdict is rendered. The activity tends to increase and become more intense with the progression of the case toward trial, peaks immediately prior to trial, and then levels-off or declines. Finally, it is contingent upon not only the issues initially perceived in the case but also those which emerge anew as the case makes its way through trial. Throughout this preparation, *the overall goal is to construct a viable defense story*: Defenders attempt to assemble as much information as possible to support the claim that the defendant is not guilty of crime and to keep out as much information as possible that suggests he or she is. As Tom explained:

> A trial consists of evidence. And my preparation consists of trying to marshal the evidence and make as much of it available to the trier of fact that will help my client, and keep as much out that will hurt my client ... [Interviewer: Do you conduct legal research?] Certainly. Tons of it. Jury instructions are an interesting one ... [Interviewer: Do you

do anything else to prepare?] You talk to witnesses. You try to get them on your side ... Building up contradictions in testimony is a big thing. Investigation. Photographs – I take a lot of photographs ... Visual aids. Jurors like to be entertained ... Physical evidence ... [Interviewer: What about preparing the witnesses?] Yeah. The more time you've got, the more time you spend. I mean when I – the best way is to write it all out. The format. And then just go down it with them. I don't script it out – I don't write out the questions and the answers but I'll write out just about everything that I'm going to ask them ... Particularly when you're dealing with a client, it's important to try to anticipate what the D.A. is going to ask.

The Defenders prepare cases for trial in both conventional and unconventional ways. Conventional methods include the performance of legal research and investigations, as well as the preparation of defense presentations. Unconventional methods include the conduct of pre-trial hearings for investigative purposes.

Conventional Modes of Preparing Cases for Trial

As indicated in Tom's comments above, one conventional way in which Defenders prepare cases for trial is through legal research. This entails an examination of the most recent case law relevant to any legal issues in the case. These issues typically concern search and seizure law as well as jury instructions. After the research has been conducted, Defenders then attempt to fit the facts of the incident to the law. In so doing, they develop arguments either for any legal procedure or finding which enhances defense rhetoric, or against any legal procedure or finding which jeopardizes the viability of that rhetoric. In essence, they are developing secondary legal stories (or sub-plots) with which to negotiate the legal format for primary evidence stories. Two Defenders explained these procedures in the following manners:

Nora: [Interviewer: Do you do some legal research for trial?] Yeah. [Interviewer: Would you explain that for me?] Well, you want to look at two main areas, I think. You want to look at the law – or the charge that your client's facing and try to find cases that help you, or say that your client somehow doesn't fall under that case, or a case that allows you to bring in a certain kind of evidence or leave out a certain kind of evidence. You want to look at the rules of evidence to see if you can use those to your advantage, or how you're gonna get around a sticky rule or problem. And you want to look at the instructions of the case which is the law of the case which is given to the jury. These are the rules and guidelines which they make a decision by. And so you want to check those out and see if there are any new twists or unusual cases that would affect your case and how you argue your case, and whether there's some unusual jury instruction you can get in, or a novel argument or unique approach to that law of the case.

Kathy: [Interviewer: How do you prepare for trial through legal research?]: You identify the issues at a trial, and you find out what the law is on those particular issues ... If there's some evidence that you want to come in in front of the jury, you have to find a way to make it admissible ... Usually evidence will fit in more than one category. A statement could be hearsay, and inadmissible. If you bring it in to show the state of mind of the person who made the statement, then that would make it admissible. So you have to determine what the issues in your case are, and how you're going to prove your case.

The argument that Defenders develop along with a statement of the facts surrounding it is then submitted in writing to a judge in the form of a 'motion'. They may also argue the motion orally in a hearing.

Investigations are another conventional manner by which Defenders prepare cases for trial. As suggested in the previous chapter, these inquiries pertain either to evidence already gathered by the D.A. or to any information which their clients report:[2]

Mindy: If there's definite witnesses, I have an investigator go talk to them. If I don't have any witnesses listed, I have the investigator look to see if there are any witnesses. I will then talk to them and find out what their version is. Depending on the case, sometimes I have character witnesses for the defendant. And I have those people interviewed, because I have to find out whether they're good witnesses ... [T]here are [also] some cases where it doesn't make any difference whether the witnesses are interviewed prior to [the preliminary hearing], and there are some cases where it makes all the difference in the world. Because you might get statements out of them ... Particularly if you feel the witness is a liar. Liars oftentimes have problems remembering what they say. If you ask them a lot of questions they can't remember them all, and then you've got something in which to compare their testimony during the preliminary hearing if they've been interviewed ahead of time. And then you can say, 'Well, on such and such date you said something to my investigator'. Makes them look bad.

Nora: I had this case the other day, I had already read it, after talking to the client I went back and read the case, and had things I wanted the investigator to follow up. I needed a diagram. I needed to know if what my client said could be verified ... [After reviewing the police report,] I talk to the defendant and he says 'Yep. That's what went on'. Or he says 'No, that's not how it happened'. And then I try to get an investigator on it.

Through investigations, Defenders attempt to obtain additional information that will enable them to construct a better defense story (or what is the same thing, enhance their rhetoric) and thereby cast doubt onto the D.A.'s evidence.

Defenders also prepare for their actual presentation of a story during trial. As Nora explained,

You prepare the direct examination of each and every witness, you prepare an opening statement, you prepare a closing statement ... And of course, you've got all your investigative reports that you have to go over and factor in and sort of cross-reference and use as a basis for all of your questions for all of your witnesses.

Preparation of defense presentations also involves instructing or 'coaching' defense witnesses on how to present themselves in front of the judge and jury. Because they will appear before the latter court actors regardless of their intentions to testify formally, Defenders also counsel their clients about their appearance. It is expected, of course, that all this instruction will bolster the defense rhetoric. As evident in the comments below, it also means that their performances should conform with traditional or status quo standards of acceptability – standards which are difficult for typical indigent defendants and their allies to emulate:

> William: The defense attorney generally has a theory [i.e., a story] which kind of pervades [the trial] ... depending on your theory, self-defense, for instance ... Many times the jury will accept the role that you are attempting to facilitate for your client [but] you have to prepare them to accept the role. [Interviewer: Does the defendant actually do anything?] Yeah. In that particular example, you would not want your client to come off as a brute. And he must *dress professional, looking nice, looking non-threatening, holds open the door for jurors, helping ladies with their chairs, treating bailiffs with due respect, and so on.* [Interviewer: Do you consult with the defendant?] Sure. We want the defendant to be completely aware of the business of trial. And we should talk about the image that he gives off. [Emphasis added.]

> Tom: [A] lot of [our clients] have emotional problems. Some of them have physical problems. Many of them simply are not intelligent – they're developmentally disabled. Others are just people who have had very unhappy, unpleasant, and sad lives. Most of them don't have much experience being in court. Nervousness is extremely common. They're very afraid to testify. They have no experience at it. *And as a result, they require a great deal of preparation to get it done right. Maybe one of the reasons why I'm reluctant to put them on. With the time constraints that I have, I cannot give them a two-week course on how to testify.* [Emphasis added.]

> Vera: I have a client right now, I'm gonna settle this case, because not only are the facts very bad – but that's not really the main problem because – the problem is that I will never be able to get this guy into a state where he can testify. In a credible, cohesive way. And I wouldn't want to put him in front of a jury unless I had the most fabulous facts in the world. [Interviewer: What's not credible and cohesive?] He doesn't know what's going on, he doesn't understand the

system ... *And* – that's not the bad part – he will not be able to handle cross-examination by the District Attorney. *In other words, I could sit with him and I could go over all the questions I'm gonna ask him, and he would be able to remember the answers, but if he had to think on his feet to a question that he wasn't prepared for* because he can't conceptualize what's going on – he doesn't understand that we're dealing with a theory of defense that has to be consistent throughout. [Emphasis added.]

A number of researchers have studied the image which defendants project and its effect on criminal case outcomes. Kalven and Zeisel (1976) and Reskin and Visher (1986), for example, found that certain of a defendant's social characteristics are likely to make a defendant more sympathetic to jurors, especially in cases where the prosecution evidence is weak. In two separate studies, Kruttschnitt (1980; 1982) found that indicators of respectability (i.e., prior criminal record, economic rank, employment status, previous psychiatric care, previous drug or alcohol abuse, employer censorship, and peer deviance) are associated with the sanctions that female criminal defendants receive. In addition, Swigert and Farrell (1977) found that a defendant's social class and conformity to a popular stereotype of criminality (i.e., the 'normal primitive') are associated with murder convictions, and Farrell (1971) found that lower-class defendants accused of homosexual offenses are more likely than their upper-class counterparts both to conform to the stereotype of homosexuality and to be detained and treated severely by criminal justice officials.

The findings presented here also indicate that Defenders expect their client's image to affect the judge and jury's behavior: regardless of their decisions to formally testify, their clients are expected to act as silent 'testaments' to themselves throughout litigation proceedings and to become part of the story which Defenders construct during a trial. These images should not be viewed as static or immutable, however. Instead, they are *constructed and managed* from an array of possibilities (see also Maynard, 1982). Nevertheless, the array is *not* unlimited. Instead, *it is circumscribed by both the dictates of common sense and defendants' cultural resources*. Thus, because indigent defendants typically lack the cultural resources with which to be portrayed in a manner convincing to middle-class judges and juries, Defenders experience some serious constraints in characterizing their clients as credible and morally upright persons *regardless of* their actual innocence or guilt.

Unconventional Modes of Preparing Cases for Trial

The unconventional ways in which Defenders prepare their cases for trial include the conduct of preliminary and motion hearings. Although these hearings are intended for other purposes (discussed below), Defenders oftentimes use them to investigate further the D.A.'s case and 'pin-down' the testimony of prosecution witnesses for later impeachment purposes:

> LuAnn: [Interviewer: What are your goals during the preliminary hearing?] Discovery. It's to give me information. My goal is to get as much information to test the witnesses out, to see how they respond to certain techniques of cross-examination, to see how they respond to my personality, to see what type of witnesses they make, what they look like. But mostly to try and get as much information as possible from them that is not in the police report, and to narrow them down on things that I want them to have specific answers on now, but that might change later. So, you know, 'What was the color of his car?' 'It was a red car'. And then at the trial, 'It was a blue car'. That's obvious and it hardly ever happens, but you're always looking for something like that.

> Kathy: [Interviewer: What is your goal throughout a motion hearing?] The goal will be to have certain evidence suppressed. A secondary goal since the first goal rarely occurs is to use it for discovery purposes – to find out as much information as you can.

Litigating Guilt Through Formal Hearings: Evidentiary Story-Telling

Taking a case to trial entails the litigation of issues throughout formal hearings. In Smith City, there are three types of hearings wherein attorneys may dispute the criminal charges in cases on the trial track. These are preliminary hearings, motion hearings and jury trials. Through any or all of these, Defenders may attempt to 'walk' their clients, or, somehow free them from further prosecution and possible sanctioning.

Preliminary and motion hearings usually occur prior to trial and are used to litigate the legality of the procedures used against the defendant, or, to debate whether the defendant's rights as specified in the Fourth and Fifth Amendments of the U.S. Constitution[3] have been upheld. A preliminary hearing is used specifically to establish whether a viable case exists against a defendant that can be taken to trial. During this hearing, the prosecution is responsible for proving 'by a preponderance of the evidence' (rather than 'beyond a reasonable doubt') that the defendant committed the crime or crimes with which he is charged and therefore that grounds exist for the continuance of the case against the defendant. If the prosecution is unsuccessful, the charges are dismissed. However, the charges may be refiled at a later date if the D.A. manages to produce stronger evidence.

The purpose of a motion hearing is to contest the legality of the method by which evidence was obtained; i.e., to contest search and seizure procedures. The burden of proof in these hearings shifts depending on whether law enforcement officials obtained a warrant prior to searching for and seizing evidence. If no warrant was obtained, it is the prosecutor's responsibility to prove 'probable cause' (or a 'reasonable suspicion') for a search. Otherwise, the defense is liable to prove there was no cause to detain and search the defendant. If the legality of the search and seizure is successfully challenged, the evidence obtained through those measures is 'suppressed', or thrown out. This frequently means *all* the evidence is thrown out and the case against the defendant is dismissed.

In jury trials, the District Attorney is responsible for proving 'beyond a reasonable doubt' that a defendant committed the crime or crimes with which he is charged. Although the defense attorney is not legally responsible for proving anything, he or she attempts at the very least to cast doubt onto the prosecutor's evidence. After the presentation of evidence during a trial, the jury may reach one of several possible types of verdicts. These are 1) that the defendant is guilty of all the criminal counts, 2) that the defendant is not guilty of all the counts, 3) that the defendant is guilty of some and not guilty of other counts, and 4) that they cannot reach a consensus on any or all of the criminal counts and are therefore 'hung'. It is only in the second instance that the defendant is set completely free.

Although certainly there are some major differences among the hearings, there are also some important similarities. Among them, all types of formal hearings involve some type of legal story-telling that leads to a conclusion regarding the defendant's guilt of crime. In addition, all are structured by similar kinds of background understandings (or story-telling frames of reference) and employ similar types of litigation procedures (or techniques for telling legal stories). The remainder of this section examines these shared dimensions of formal litigation hearings.

Background Understandings: The Story-Telling Frame of Reference

A number of sociologists have found that social life is structured by tacit, taken-for-granted background understandings.[4] Likewise, formal litigation proceedings are structured by the attorneys' largely unspoken awareness of the relevant laws and legal procedures for the hearing,[5] witnesses' prior accounts of incidents (or the evidence story which is likely to be told) and common sense.

Two sorts of legal codes structure the Defenders' behavior during court proceedings. These are the law(s) which one of the attorneys is liable to corroborate (e.g., a penal code or Constitutional principle) and rules of evidence.

Regarding the first, an understanding of the precise elements of the relevant law structures the presentation of evidence and examination of witnesses throughout the hearing. For example, the D.A. is responsible for proving in preliminary hearings and jury trials that all the elements of all those crimes with which the defendant is charged *and* are formally specified in the penal code were manifested in the defendant's behavior. Conversely, the Defender is liable to suggest that the D.A. has not proven such contentions. Based upon this shared understanding, each of the attorneys attempts to present or impugn evidence stories through the testimony of witnesses.

'Rules of Evidence' are legal codes that define what types of information are permissible *as* evidence in a court setting. During a formal hearing, these understandings structure the manner in which attorneys raise 'objections' by providing their legal basis. Defenders raise objections not simply because prosecution testimony does not conform to proper legal format, however, but more importantly to keep information which could harm the defendant out of a proceeding. Nevertheless, because they usually want to hear everything that prosecution witnesses have to say during pre-trial hearings, they tend to raise fewer objections in these hearings than they do during jury trials.[6] Another reason why Defenders raise objections is to create a record of issues for possible appeal later on.

In his study on juvenile justice in three cities, Cicourel (1968) found that previously developed theories about the nature of a juvenile case structure court hearings. These theories form important background understandings and officials attempt to elicit information from witnesses to substantiate these theories. Similarly, knowledge of witnesses' prior accounts as ascertained through police reports and previous investigations (or the evidence story which is expected to be told) as well as taken-for-granted commonsense

understandings of what constitutes credible testimony form important
background understandings for Defenders throughout formal litigation
proceedings. There are three major reasons for this. First, because the
prosecution story comprises 'the case against the defendant', Defenders must
orient their lines-of-questioning toward these accounts in an attempt to
impeach witnesses. Second, Defenders must base their lines-of-questioning on
the prior accounts of both defense and prosecution witnesses in order to tell
or construct their own evidence story. Finally, taken-for-granted
commonsense understandings of what constitute (culturally) 'plausible'
accounts enables Defenders to impeach or construct credible evidence stories
in both instances.

The taken-for-granted background understandings which structure court
hearings can be seen in Kathy's description of what she expects during her
upcoming trial:

> *The D.A. says that the evidence will show* that my client on
> four separate occasions molested his step-daughter [i.e., that
> the defendant committed the crime of child sexual abuse].
> And he has what he says is physical evidence to show that.
> And this is one case where I will not be able to show beyond
> a reasonable doubt that my guy didn't do it. This is a real
> reasonable doubt case. I will bring in my own experts to
> evaluate the medical evidence *to show that the physical
> evidence does not support the D.A.'s contention and does not
> support the complaining witness's statements.* [Emphasis
> added.]

Like Kathy's comments, Janet's remarks presuppose the commonsense
understanding that there is only one objective and intersubjective world and
that a jury should therefore conclude that when two inconsistent accounts of
reality are offered, one account – preferably the prosecutor's – is false:

> [I]f it's a case where there's any possibility of going to trial,
> the most important thing is to get as much information as you
> can [during a preliminary hearing]. Get every detail. Pin the
> witnesses down to what they say happened. Pin them down
> as to what they say, what they put in their report, so that later
> on during trial they cannot all of a sudden come up with
> something new ... And you can always go back and say 'Isn't
> it true when I asked you during the preliminary hearing about

your report, you said it was accurate, everything was in there. And now all of a sudden you've come up with this'.

Conducting the Formal Litigation Proceedings: Techniques for Evidentiary Story-Telling

A formal litigation (or legal story-telling) proceeding unfolds in a linear progression that consists of three phases: the beginning phase, the evidentiary phase, and the phase of conclusion. The beginning phase includes some sort of introduction to the criminal case being litigated. It also tends to include some sort of inquiry by the judge concerning the general plan of the hearing, statements on the part of the attorneys concerning their preparedness, and perhaps some motions. The beginning phase of a jury trial also includes *voir dire* (or jury selection) as well as opening statements whereby both the prosecution and defense describe their cases 'in chief', or, what they maintain the evidence will or will not show through the stories being told in court.

In the evidentiary phase, both attorneys actually present their cases. Whichever attorney is responsible for proving a contention goes first. This is usually the D.A. After examining the first witness, the attorney for the other side may then cross-examine him or her.[7] After both sides have examined and cross-examined the witness to their satisfaction, the next witness is called and the same process of examination and cross-examination is repeated. This continues until all witnesses for the first attorney have testified. It is then the second attorney's turn to present a case and the same procedures are followed. However, it is not mandatory for the second attorney to present a separate case. Rather, he or she may opt simply to cast doubt through the cross-examination of the first attorney's witnesses. Regardless, he or she still tells an evidence story insofar as he or she attempts to assert claims that counter the first attorney's.

The conclusion phase consists most importantly of the rendering of some type of decision or verdict. It may also entail setting dates and times for future proceedings as well as perhaps a very brief motion or two. In a jury trial, it also consists of closing arguments whereby the attorneys recap the stories they told or the cases they presented.

The remainder of this section focuses upon the evidentiary phase of one formal litigation proceeding. In examining this proceeding, we will employ Kenneth Burke's dramatistic 'pentad'. The pentad consists of five key terms that are basic forms of thought (or ways of thinking) necessarily implicated in the process of defining situations (Burke, 1969; Gusfield, 1991). The five terms are Act, Scene, Agent, Agency, and Purpose. While all five terms are implicated in definitions of situations, Burke argues that any language system (or cultural domain of meaning) may emphasize one or more over others in providing explanations of behavior. For our purposes, it is relevant not merely that the five key terms are implicated in definitions of situations, but that the language system of common sense limits the specific vocabulary and possible rhetoric one can employ for defining situations. In other words, common sense is a type of terministic screen or cultural grammar that constrains the manners in which social actors can view as well as talk about situations.

The preliminary hearing examined below concerns a burglary case. The D.A. had previously dismissed the case prior to the hearing because a key prosecution witness failed to appear. However, the failure to appear was apparently due to the witness's misunderstanding, and the case was refiled after the misunderstanding was cleared up.

The defendant in the case was a relatively tall, thin black male who appeared to be in his late 30s or early 40s. With the exception of some broken front teeth, he was a rather attractive man. He was also from another state, homeless, had no relatives in the area, and had only been in the area approximately two weeks prior to his arrest. As surmised beforehand by the Defender who handled the case, the defendant also had a drinking problem.

The police report stated that police officers caught the defendant inside a warehouse shortly after the night watchman, who lived in and worked for the warehouse, phoned in a burglary. The defendant stated that he was inside the building only to use the bathroom. He insisted that he had received permission to use the bathroom from the night watchman, and apparently the night watchman – who was an older man of retirement age – forgot that he was in the building for that purpose. Because he was discovered inside the warehouse after the burglary had been reported and while the police were taking the report from the night watchman, the prosecution alleged that the defendant was a burglar.

Because the defendant told his attorney that he had no prior record other than drunkenness (which eventually turned out to be untrue) and because the police report all-too-conspicuously related how the prosecution witnesses were careful to lock the door every time an exit or entry took place, the Defender decided the case was triable. Upon concluding this, the Defender sent out an investigator to talk with the night watchman in order to ascertain more clearly what his account of the incident was and what type of witness he would be. As later reported to the Defender, the night watchman was an older man who appeared to have some problems remembering things. In fact, it was speculated that the case was dismissed previously because this witness had forgotten the date and time of the previously scheduled preliminary hearing.

The D.A.'s Case Against the Defendant The D.A. in this hearing was responsible for proving by a preponderance of the evidence that the defendant committed the act of burglary. Burglary is defined as 'illegal entry with the intent to commit theft or some felony'. This understanding of the law prescribed to the D.A. what information he needed to produce (or what type of plot he needed to develop) in order to prove his case. This information was elicited from a witness. The following excerpts are from the court transcript of the preliminary hearing. The D.A. posed all questions and his first witness, who was the night watchman at the business, provided all answers:

> Q: Mr. [Witness], back on April 13,1985, where were you living at that time?
>
> A: Living at 2222 'Z' Street. 2222 'Z' street.
>
> Q: Now, is that a home or is that some type of business?
>
> A: It is a business. For the automotive delivery service.
>
> (...)
>
> Q: What time did the last person [other than himself] leave that day?
>
> A: The last person left at approximately 3:00 o'clock.
>
> Q: And at 3:00 o'clock did you secure the place of business?
>
> A: Yes.
>
> (...)
>
> Q: Sometime that night, did you leave your place of business?
>
> A: Yes, I did.

Q: What time was it that you left?

A: Approximately 9:00 o'clock.

(...)

Q: What did you do after [un]locking the door [upon your return]?

A: Well, I walked to the back of the building where my office is and where I spend my time. And as I entered the office door, I noticed that there was a box of [business] cards that were sitting on the desk, which I knew I didn't put them there. Then, I noticed there were desk drawers open, and I also had 2 suitcases and they were both open. They were cracked, so I knew that someone had ransacked my office.

Q: Had these items been in that condition when you left at 9:00 o'clock?

A: No.

(...)

Q: While you were talking to [the manager] on the telephone, did you notice anything unusual at that point in time?

A: Yes. I noticed that the window in the front of the building had been broken out and that there was boxes sitting in the trough where the large sliding door has to open. The boxes had been put in that area, and this was when I noticed the window had been broken.

Q: Now, this window that had been broken, had it been broken earlier in the evening before you left at 9:00 o'clock?

A: No.

(...)

Q: After the police officer took his report, did something else happen inside the building?

A: Well, the police officer made the remark that there is a possibility that someone might still be here and about that time I turned around and started to walk out of the office. And at that time, I saw someone coming out of the front office, which is at the front of the building right beside the small door. There is an office off to your left, and that person was coming out of that office and reaching for the small door to get out.

(...)

Q: What exactly was this person doing when you saw this person for the first time?

A: Reaching out for the door, trying to tiptoe, reaching for the door. I assume he was trying to reach for the door and get out.

(...)

Q: Now, this person that was arrested inside your building, do you see him in court today?

A: Yes. I do.

(...)

Q: This person that you have just identified, did you give that person permission to be inside the building before that night?
A: No.

Q: Had you ever seen that person before?

A: No, I had not seen him.

Mr. D.A.: I have no further questions.

In this example, the D.A. suggests through his first witness that the defendant, who is defined as a 'stranger', entered a business establishment in a very 'inappropriate' way at a very 'inappropriate' time, and handled property in the business in an 'inappropriate' manner. The D.A. adds that the defendant did not have explicit permission to be in the building and that he attempted to exit the building in a very 'unusual' or atypical manner. In other words, the D.A. suggests through his witness that the defendant entered a business establishment illegally with the intent to commit theft. It is important to point out here that *the D.A.'s innuendos only make sense within the tacit, taken-for-granted, cultural context of 'common sense'*: unable to recognize the context, members of some other culture may not discern anything wrong with the defendant's behavior.

In employing Burke's pentad to understand the interaction, we find that the *scene* is defined as a 'business establishment'. This term implies a number of other defining features. Specifically, it prescribes what *agents* have tacit permission to act in *what manners* (i.e., *agency*) and for what *purposes*. It also implies inappropriate behavior. Consequently, the D.A.'s witness does not have to explain why the defendant's behavior is inappropriate. He simply has to describe the scene (a business), the agent (a stranger), the acts (entry and ransacking) and the agency (through the window). Without further ado, the defendant's motive is then simply understood. Again, this understanding occurs only within the cultural idiom of common sense.

It is also important to point out here that the D.A. in this case did not question or need to 'explain' who actually owned the structure and the property being guarded and, therefore, who did and did not have the right to enter the structure and confiscate property. It would not matter in this case, for example, that the night watchman was guarding property for someone not entitled to it – whether legally or in some other, perhaps Marxist, sense. While one might assert that the D.A. had 'no reason' to question such entitlements, such logic and related assumptions illustrate the very point being made here: *common sense is a terministic screen or cultural grammar that prescribes one way of viewing reality at the same time it proscribes alternative manners of viewing the situation.* The D.A. merely assumed (and was required *only* to assume) that behaviors that conform to common sense terms are correct and legitimate, while those that do not are not correct or legitimate. Moreover and perhaps most importantly, this example illustrates how the grammar and rhetoric of common sense in our society favors those who maintain control over (or 'own') property over those who do not.[8] As Ewick and Silbey (1995) argue, it is the unarticulated and unexamined 'plausibility' of the story that results in hegemony.

The Defense Case The Defender's official goal during a preliminary hearing is to cast doubt onto the D.A.'s evidence. This means he or she must create uncertainty regarding any one or all of the components of the hypothesis that the D.A. must prove. Thus, if the D.A. is liable to prove that the defendant committed the act of burglary, the Defender attempts to elicit information which casts doubt as to whether 1) a crime (either entirely or in part) was committed, 2) the defendant committed that crime, or 3) both. As Amsterdam and Bruner (2000: 117) indicate, these are the obligatory plots of defense stories.

In casting doubt, the Defender attempts to *normalize* the defendant's alleged inappropriate behavior. He does this by eliciting other, previously disregarded *yet commonsense* information, which then modifies the context for understanding the earlier constructed behavior patterns. This somewhat amended definition of the situation makes the previously constructed behavior patterns now seem routine and acceptable. It is important to emphasize here that, like the D.A.'s behavior, the Defender's strategy presupposes shared cultural understandings regarding 'normal' and 'appropriate' behavior; i.e., it presupposes 'common sense'. This is illustrated in the following excerpts from the same preliminary hearing. The Defender posed all questions and the same witness provided all answers as previously:

> Q: These boxes that you refer to that were near the window, were these boxes that contained automotive supplies?
>
> A: Yes.
>
> Q: So these are boxes that belong to your establishment; is that correct?
>
> A: Right.
>
> (...)
>
> Q: This evening had you been gone for approximately an hour and a half?
>
> A: Yes. Right.
>
> Q: At the time that you left, did you inspect the premises?

A: Inspect the premises?

Q: Yes. Did you look around, make sure everything was all right?

A: No. I didn't look around. I just got up and walked out like I usually do.

(...)

Q: You didn't notice those boxes when you left that evening; is that true?

A: I didn't notice them; what do you mean?

Q: You didn't notice them when you walked out of the door to leave at 9:00 o'clock?

A: I couldn't say that I paid any particular attention to those boxes, no. Like I said, I got from the back room and went through the door and locked it, and that's it.

Q: At 10:30 when you came back, you didn't notice the boxes either?

A: No. I didn't notice them when I first came in the building.

Q: If you could have looked as you walked in the door, you could have easily seen them; couldn't you?

A: Yes.

(...)

Q: And when you came back in, the first thing you noticed was that your office in the back looked like somebody had been there while you were gone?

A: That was the first indication that I noticed that someone had ransacked it.

Q: You don't know whether in that hour and a half another employee of the place had come in and maybe looked through [your property], for example?

A: I sure don't.

(...)

Q: Did it look like any of [your property was] missing?

A: No.

Q: Was anything missing at all?

A: I did not know anything was missing, no.

Q: As of this date, you still are not aware of anything missing?

A: Nothing, correct.

(...)

Q: And [when the police officer] came back through the door. Where did you go with him?

A: To the rear of the building. Back to my small office.

Q: That was when the suggestion was made by the officer that the person still might be there?
A: Yes.

Q: Did you hear somebody yelling to you about that point?

A: No, I didn't.

(...)

Q: When you saw this individual coming out of the office, did you actually see him coming outside of the office?
A: He came with us outside of the office.

Q: So you assumed he was coming out of that office?

A: Yeah, okay.

(...)

Q: Did you ever see him get his hand on that door?

A: He didn't get to the door.

Q: Why didn't he get to the door?

A: Because I yelled out and the policemen came out and arrested him before he got to the door.

Q: Did you see him being searched?

A: Yes.

Q: Was anything recovered from him that belonged to the business?

A: No.

Q: You never saw him with any of the property that belonged to the business, did you?

A: No.

Q: Do you have a bathroom located in the business?

A: Yes.

Q: Where is that bathroom located?

A: For instance, my office is here. The bathroom is to the right [gesturing] about 10 feet.

Q: Near the back of the building; is that correct?

A: Right.

Mr. Defense Attorney: I have nothing further.

By eliciting additional information from the D.A.'s witness, the Defender attempted to shed a different light on the patterns previously constructed by the D.A. Specifically, he suggests that there is nothing unusual about boxes alongside the window of a warehouse and that perhaps their position was a simple matter of routine disarray. Similarly, by establishing that no property from the business was recovered from the defendant and that the night watchman does not know whether an employee might have instead sifted through his possessions, he suggests there is little reason to believe the defendant handled another's property inappropriately. Finally, because he establishes that the defendant was found near the bathroom and not actually leaving an office of the warehouse, the Defender also suggests that perhaps the defendant actually had a legitimate reason for being in the warehouse. In other words, he suggests it is doubtful that the defendant illegally entered the business with the intent to commit theft; i.e., that the defendant committed burglary.

Employing Burke's pentad to this situation, we should first note that the Defender continues to employ the language or symbolic system of common sense: he does not dispute whether the scene is actually a business establishment nor does he question whether the defendant's alleged behavior is inappropriate. He *could* have argued, for example, that the assumed business was 'actually' God's temple and that the defendant was merely attempting to gain entry in the sacredly ordained fashion. Instead, he attempts to redefine the defendant's motives by emphasizing other agents (i.e., warehouse employees) and acts (i.e., using the bathroom and the routinely unkempt character of warehouses) *that are consistent with the commonsense definition of the situation.*

It is also critical to point out here that like the D.A., the Defender did not question who actually owned the property at issue and whether they were actually entitled to it. Neither did he attempt to suggest either that the business enterprise behaved inappropriately by failing to provide some basic needs for a poor, homeless person or that it was appropriate for a poor, homeless person to enter into the business establishment in order to fulfill some basic needs. Instead, because of their incongruity with common sense, it was merely assumed that these latter rights and obligations do not exist. Consequently, the grammar and rhetoric of common sense can once again be seen to favor the propertied and powerful over those less fortunate: if you have it, you are not assumed to be obligated to share it, and if you do not have it, you are assumed to have no right to a portion of it.

A strategy that is essentially the same as that employed by Karl in the preliminary hearing described above is illustrated in the following account provided by LuAnn:

> [Interviewer: How do you typically attempt to impeach the D.A.'s evidence?] Well, through cross-examination. A few well-chosen questions ... [Y]ou try to show that everybody, and this works with juries – they really like this, that people are talking in conclusionary terms. [For example,] 'Well, I knew he was breaking into this car.' 'How did you know?' 'Because he was in this car, rummaging around in this car.' 'Did you see him break in?' 'No.' 'The first time you saw the man was in the car, wasn't it?' 'Yes.' 'He was sitting in the passenger seat and you thought that was unusual, didn't you?' 'Yeah.' 'And he was looking through some papers, is that right?' 'Right.' 'Was he sweating?' 'No.' 'Was he making any noises?' 'No.' 'Did he keep looking over his shoulder?' 'No.' 'He was just involved with what he was doing, is that right? So you thought that was unusual?' 'Yes.' 'Well, what else was unusual?' 'Well, the way he was dressed.' 'Why?' 'Because this is [a wealthy area] and everybody wears coats and ties. I mean it's my favorite dress. And this black guy shouldn't have been there in this art gallery's parking lot wearing a shabby little jacket with a cap.' And it wasn't just because he was black, of course, because she thought he was a good-looking man – probably because he had white features, but you just show how she concluded from the fact that he was not in a suit and tie, that he was on the passenger's side of the vehicle, and that he was looking through papers [that she concludes that] he had no business being inside of that car. And that he had broken into the car. That obviously the car had not been left unlocked. He'd broken into it. The truth of the matter is no one saw

him break into it. She thought he had no business being there
– and maybe he did and maybe he didn't, if he was there at
all. But nothing was taken from the car. And there's no point
of entry. There's no pry marks. There's no slim jim. The car
was left open. Maybe he did in fact rummage through it, but
he didn't take anything. Maybe he didn't break in with the
intent to steal. And maybe he made a mistake – that he
thought it was his car. Maybe a lot of things.

As already suggested, jury trials are more extensive than preliminary and
motion hearings. Re-direct and re-cross examinations, as well as further
re-direct and further re-cross examinations, for example, are common during
a jury trial. And, due at least partially to the fact that Defenders do not feel
pressured to conceal their case from the D.A., more witnesses are called and
examined. Motion hearings, on the other hand, are more abridged than either
jury trials or preliminary hearings.

Defenders also conduct trial proceedings in a more straight-forward,
calculated manner than preliminary or motion hearings. In the preliminary
hearing described above, for example, the Defender was on a kind of 'fishing
expedition' whereby he hoped to uncover details that would help him better
prepare the case for trial. In contrast, the Defender's lines-of-questioning
during a trial are more carefully prepared and tailored to substantiate a single,
coherent, and consistent defense story.

Conclusion

Upon deciding to take a case to trial, Defenders attempt to build a viable
defense story: they research, apply and argue all case law which they believe
will benefit their clients, seek out exculpating information through both
legitimate as well as somewhat dubious investigative techniques, and prepare
themselves as well as other defense allies for their courtroom presentations.
Forearmed with relevant information, they then endeavor to persuade the
judge and jury that the defendant should not be found guilty of a crime. In
other words, they carefully and zealously defend their clients at trial and
thereby provide them with what appears to be just representation.

Nevertheless, while their professional behavior appears rigorous and fair,
Defenders experience various types of cultural constraints in defending their
clients. First and foremost, the cultural idiom of common sense limits the

manner in which reality can be defined and the way evidence stories can be told in the first place. As Amsterdam and Bruner state,

> [O]ur very success in making things narratively believable often seduces us into unintended conventional stances toward the world (2000: 113).

This means that status quo definitions of reality prevail and that people who violate the norms of the powerful are viewed suspiciously *even when they have committed no crime*. Second, because the lifestyles and characteristics of typical indigent defendants and their personal allies do not conform to traditional, status quo standards of respectability, Defenders are less able to build viable defense stories on their behalf. Among other things, this means that indigent defendants tend to be less credible 'testaments' to themselves regardless of whether they formally take the witness stand and (again) *regardless of their actual guilt of crime*. Finally, although Defenders negotiate the legal format of evidence stories, because they must marshal evidence with regard to specific laws and work within the confines of law in order to challenge the prosecutor's case, the cultural idiom of the attorneys' legal expertise makes it possible for the defendant's behavior to be defined as 'criminal' in any instance.[9] Thus, not only do poor criminal suspects experience greater disadvantages in taking their cases to trial and are therefore more likely to be convicted for crimes than other types of defendants, but the legal system plays an instrumental role in maintaining class inequities by stigmatizing those who violate the norms of the powerful.

Notes

1   Among researchers, Sudnow (1965) indicated that Public Defenders conduct trials in an unenthusiastic, routine manner that is largely geared to substantiate the D.A'.s contentions and at the same time placate stubborn defendants who refuse to plea bargain. Similarly, Blumberg (1967b) has found that the quality of overall advocacy provided by defense attorneys is contingent on the size of the fee that an attorney receives. By implication, Blumberg suggests that attorneys for the poor provide a relatively low quality of advocacy for their clients. Similar sentiments are reflected in certain of the observations of Clarke and Koch (1976), Farrell (1971), Holmes et al (1987) and Swigert and Farrell (1977).

2   Most of this investigation is done by outside detective agencies that work in close consultation with the Defenders.

3   According to the Fifth Amendment of the U.S. Constitution, 'No person shall be held to answer for a capital, or otherwise infamous, crime, *unless on a presentment or indictment of a grand jury ...* [Emphasis added.]' The preliminary hearing commonly takes the place of a Grand Jury and is intended to safeguard a person's Fifth Amendment rights. If during

a preliminary hearing the District Attorney is unable to prove to a judge by a preponderance of the evidence that the defendant committed the crime(s) with which he is charged, it is assumed that to continue with the criminal proceedings against the defendant would be illegal, or, a violation of the defendant's Fifth Amendment rights.

According to the Fourth Amendment of the U.S. Constitution, 'The right of the people to be secure in their persons, houses, papers, and effects, against unreasonable searches and seizures, shall not be violated; and no warrants shall issue, but upon probable cause, supported by oath or affirmation, and particularly describing the place to be searched and the persons or things to be seized'. As may be apparent, a defendant's Fourth Amendment rights involve 'Search and Seizure' issues. While separate motion hearings are typically used to litigate these matters, preliminary hearings are also sometimes used to argue motions to dismiss a case based on Fourth Amendment issues.

4   See for example, Berger and Luckmann (1967), Cicourel (1968), Garfinkle (1967), and Mehan and Wood (1975).

5   See also, Maroules (1986).

6   Several Defenders stated that they also object to matters sometimes simply to disrupt the 'flow' of the D.A.'s behavior. However, during jury trials especially, Defenders are concerned that they do not appear to be hiding something from the jury. Thus, in these proceedings, carefully placed objections and their legal grounds are more important to the Defender. This also illustrates that defense rhetoric goes beyond mere oral testimony and includes the entire courtroom drama.

7   The defendant may, of course, be presented as a witness at times.

8   As Carrier (1982) argues, because Burke insists that humans are symbolic creatures, his dramatism precludes the Marxist notion that material conditions shape social existence. However, it does not preclude the mode of production as an important factor in social life. Instead, Burke finds that language systems result from the division of labor and reflect existing power relations – even though these latter social conditions are themselves the product of symbolic action. Consequently, from a dramatistic perspective, property ownership and the social relations of production are expressed in the grammar and rhetoric of social action.

9   As Amsterdam and Bruner (2000) relate, the legal system has the fundamental role of categorizing people and behavior as 'criminal' or making distinctions between 'good' and 'evil' in society.

Chapter 5

Negotiating Plea Bargains

Plea bargains and trials are frequently conceptualized in opposing terms: jury trials are thought to epitomize the ideal of justice while plea bargains are viewed as a gross corruption of justice. In an effort to assess whether one mode of case disposition is actually any more equitable than the other for poor defendants, we investigate in this chapter how Defenders negotiate the terms of plea bargains. I begin by providing a brief overview of the plea bargaining system in Smith City. I then proceed to describe the process by which Defenders plea bargain criminal cases.

An Overview of Smith City's Plea Bargaining System

In Smith City, a 'plea bargain' is an agreement made between the prosecuting attorney and the defendant (usually through the defendant's attorney) which stipulates that the defendant will plead guilty to or not contest a fixed number of criminal charges in exchange for some sort of reduction in the number and/or the seriousness of the original criminal charges. Although the Smith City District Attorney maintains that he does not do sentence bargaining, any reduction in the number or the seriousness of the original charges lodged against the defendant implies exposure to less severe sentences.[1] In addition, there is one stipulation frequently added to plea bargains that refers to the District Attorney's lack of opposition to custody spent in the local jail rather than the state prison. This stipulation is represented in agreements by the acronym 'N.O.L.T.', which means 'no opposition to local time'.

Like judges in some other jurisdictions, Smith City judges are encouraged to facilitate case settlements.[2] Consequently, when the prosecutor and Defender agree on the terms of plea bargains, judges generally accept those terms.[3] When these court actors encounter problems in reaching agreements, however, judges act as arbiters. In this arbitration, the judge typically exerts pressure on or makes promises regarding sentencing to either attorney in order to reach a settlement.

As may be apparent, plea bargain negotiations in Smith City usually involve the defense attorney, prosecuting attorney, judge, and defendant. They may at times also involve co–defendants and (even more rarely) an alleged victim. Regardless of whom they involve, however, never do the Defenders carry out all aspects of plea-bargaining in the presence of all the actors involved. Instead, their activity among prosecution allies and the judge is usually separated in time and space from their activity among defense allies.

Plea bargains in Smith City are also negotiated almost anywhere and at almost any time throughout the life of an ongoing criminal case. It most obviously occurs on the date of scheduled settlement hearings whereby one can observe blatant negotiating behavior in the judge's chambers, in the hallways outside of courtrooms, and/or in the courthouse 'holding tanks' where incarcerated defendants await scheduled court appearances. However, as will be discussed below, plea bargains may also be deliberately and clandestinely negotiated before, during, or after other types of court hearings.

Wherever or whenever plea-bargaining takes place, their successful negotiation is always followed by a public hearing wherein the agreement is formalized and officially sanctioned.

The Negotiation Process

The Defenders' goal throughout the course of any criminal case is to mitigate the harm that could befall a defendant. They maintain that because the prosecutor typically makes acceptable offers for guilty pleas or drops the charges in cases where the evidence is very weak, trials are rare and plea bargains are the most likely method through which they seek their goal. Nevertheless, although plea-bargaining is the most common method for case disposal, immediate settlement of a case is always considered in light of 'proceeding further'.

'Proceeding further' means that, until an attorney achieves acceptable settlement terms, he or she proceeds to litigate a case throughout various court hearings that could ultimately result in a jury trial and then sentencing.[4] Defenders consider their clients' cases in light of proceeding further because they perceive that better terms may be forthcoming later on in the adjudication process. Thus, many cases are not settled immediately, some cases involve multiple episodes of negotiation, and the negotiation of acceptable terms for case settlements sometimes entails a wide range of formal litigation proceedings.[5]

Defenders negotiate plea bargains through three types of activities. These are 1) assessing the D.A.'s offer for a guilty plea, 2) negotiating the terms of settlement, and 3) counseling the defendant and deciding on a course of action. While these activities are inter-related, they do not necessarily emerge in the sequence presented here and they may be more apparent at some times than at others. Sometimes Defenders counsel their clients prior to intercepting an actual offer, for example, and sometimes they negotiate the terms of a plea bargain before conferring with a client. In addition, sometimes the Defender makes an offer himself and the D.A.'s acceptance of it precludes any subsequent need for assessment as well as perhaps any further negotiation. Regardless of the order in which they occur, however, the Defenders always consider the bid for a guilty plea, always confirm the terms of a plea bargain through some type of negotiation technique, and always counsel the defendant prior to deciding on a course of action.[6]

Assessing the D.A.'s Offer for a Guilty Plea

Assessing the offer for a guilty plea entails two types of evaluations. The first involves the Defenders' understanding of the 'value of a case'. The second involves matters associated with the temporary postponement of settlement. Ultimately, both types of evaluations involve consideration of whether a case should proceed further. Thus, while Maynard (1984b) argues that case disposition delays are bargaining strategies, they can also be seen to constitute part of the defense attorney's tacit repertoire of strategies that they contemplate *prior to and apart from* interactional negotiation.

Assessing the Offer in Light of 'the Value of a Case' In assessing the D.A.'s offer for a guilty plea, the Defenders rely upon their understanding of 'the value of a case'. As discussed in Chapter Three, assessments regarding the value of a case indicate what offer or reduction in penalties Defenders should expect to receive in exchange for their client's guilty plea.[7] Based on this understanding, they assess the *actual* offer. The issue in this assessment is *not* whether the D.A. offers any reduction whatsoever in potential costs incurred by the defendant, but instead whether the reduction is 'fair' or 'reasonable' given the value of the case.[8] If it is not, they deem it unacceptable. As explained by Mindy,

> [A] first time [auto theft] is worth a misdemeanor. They might not give it to you. They might not offer it to you. But that's all its worth ... If [the D.A. says] we'll offer you a felony and we won't oppose local time, that's an offer where you can say, 'Stuff it'. Because there's no reason not to go to trial on that offer. Because if your guy loses after trial, if he's a first time offender he's not gonna be hurt. So they haven't offered you anything. [Interviewer: How do you know he's

not going to be hurt?] Because there's not a judge around
here who's gonna give prison on first offense auto theft.

As Mindy's comments suggest, when an offer is deemed 'unreasonable',
the Defenders tentatively conclude that a case should proceed further rather
than settle immediately.

Assessing the Offer in Light of Temporary Postponement   Even when the D.A.
makes a reasonable offer for a guilty plea, the Defenders consider whether an
offer might get better further along in the adjudication process. Among other
matters, they consider whether a subsequent D.A. or judge is more lenient.[9]
As Janet explained:

> If the offer can't get worse – and you know that because
> you've been doing [plea bargains] for awhile [and] you know
> what the standard offers are – the question then sometimes
> becomes are you judge shopping. Is it better to take the offer
> now because you have this particular judge that you're in
> front of, or is it better to wait 'til later when they're probably
> gonna make you the same offer, and have that judge sentence
> you? ... It also depends on who the District Attorney is in that
> department who's settling the cases. I think I mentioned
> before that sometimes that District Attorney who is kind of
> like a boss – a higher-up person in the D.A.'s office who's
> handing out all the offers – gets burned-out and the offers get
> real bad.

All other things being equal, Defenders believe that unless an initial offer
is better than average, offers for guilty pleas will not get any worse and could
become more beneficial to the defendant further along in the adjudication
process. They explain that this occurs because either the prosecutor loses
witnesses or better evidence eventually turns-up on behalf of the defense. As
explained by Robert,

> [Plea bargaining is] pretty similar [in municipal and superior
> courts]. Personalities are different. You have a different
> prosecutor and a different judge. And that often makes a
> difference ... Then there's always the possibility that you've
> developed some additional information during the interim
> that effects how you're gonna plead. First, what the offer

might be, then also evaluating the offer ... [W]hat the prosecutor tells you is that the deals are never going to get any better. [That the] inducement to plead early is that that's the best deal you're going to get, and it's going to get tougher on you if you proceed further. In fact, it doesn't seem to be the case. The defendant can get pretty much the same deal [in superior court] – although there are no guarantees about that.

Nevertheless, sometimes the prosecution case gets stronger further along in the litigation process, and the prosecutor will offer a defendant less incentive to plead guilty than previously. As Janet lamented,

[Interviewer: Do plea bargains tend to get better in superior court?] It depends ... For example, I have a case now, I think the client was offered local time [in municipal court]. They just came up with two prison priors on this guy. He swears they aren't his. I don't believe him. I think they're his. I'm afraid they're his. In which case the deal's gonna get a lot worse. So he's gonna go to trial. And that's okay. But a lot of times they do get better. [Interviewer: Most of the time?] They don't usually get worse. They very rarely get worse. They usually either stay the same or get better.

When the Defenders deduce that the offer for a guilty plea either will not or could not get any worse but could get better, they tentatively conclude that the defendant should proceed further with the case. No final conclusion is reached until after they counsel the client, however. The details of this interaction and its possible outcomes are discussed later in this chapter.

Negotiating the Terms of Plea Bargains

Before any formal agreement to settle a case is signed, the actual terms of a plea bargain are corroborated or confirmed. Employing the cultural idioms of their legal expertise and common sense, the Defenders do this through various types of negotiation techniques.

In his study on misdemeanor plea bargaining, Maynard (1984a; 1984b) examines plea bargain negotiations as a discourse phenomenon. He finds that some negotiations (i.e., unilateral opportunity negotiations) involve very little verbal maneuvering and appear to involve a 'concerting of expectations', or, the ability of participants to read situations similarly and infer mutually acceptable resolutions. Other negotiations (i.e., bilateral opportunity and compromise negotiations) involve less consensus and more verbal maneuvering. In addition, delays through continuances or the setting of trial dates are important bargaining strategies used by attorneys to mitigate or enhance a defendant's penalty.

In a related study, Maynard (1988) also finds that some negotiations involve no narratives. These cases result in routine processing. Others include narrative components or subcomponents that assess character, dispute facts or argue subjectivity.

Although they handle primarily felony cases, the Defenders' negotiating behavior appears to be largely consistent with Maynard's characterizations of misdemeanor plea bargaining: many of their negotiations involve no narrative and an apparent concerting of expectations while other negotiations entail less consensus and more narrative. The Defenders also use impending litigation proceedings as a bargaining strategy.

However, the Defenders' behavior appears to diverge from Maynard's characterization of plea bargaining in three ways. First, the Defenders' *tacit, taken-for-granted understanding of the value of a case* can be seen to structure their negotiation techniques.[10] Second, instead of continuances and the setting of trial dates, the Defenders use the somewhat veiled threat of proceeding further as a bargaining tool *during* negotiations. In other words, issues related to further case litigation are incorporated into their discourse as caveats to increase bargaining leverage. Third, the Defenders also negotiate the terms of plea bargains by making good on their threats and using other types of litigation proceedings to engender more acceptable terms for guilty pleas.

When an offer for a guilty plea is better than expected, the Defenders typically engage in 'implicit bargaining' (Mather, 1979), 'routine processing' (Maynard, 1988), or 'consensus bargaining' (Eisenstein et al, 1988). This means they accept the offer with little or no comment. However, as suggested earlier, there is an unspoken understanding that the offer is acceptable *given the value of the case.* As explained by Robert,

> [Interviewer: How do you typically plea bargain a case?]
> Well, it depends on what the offer is and what the case of the D.A. is and who the judge is. But having said all that, essentially the D.A. makes you an offer [tape ended]. It is rare, but on occasion the offer is much lower, a better offer *than you expected*. In which case, grab it. Usually, almost always you hope that it could be better. [Emphasis added.]

When an offer for a guilty plea is not better than average, the Defenders typically engage in 'explicit bargaining' (Mather, 1979). Explicit bargaining means that attorneys openly negotiate the terms of plea bargains.[11]

The Defenders' goal in explicit bargaining is to persuade the prosecutor and perhaps the judge to make a more acceptable offer for a guilty plea. One way in which they do this is by *negotiating the value of a case.*

Negotiating the value of a case does not mean that negotiation participants review all information pertinent to determining the value of a case, or that specific information is always discussed.[12] Instead, it means that the Defenders engage in a type of 'information control' (Goffman 1963) in order to evoke a more positive assessment of the value of their client's case. More specifically, they informally emphasize, overstate, de-emphasize, ignore or perhaps even put forth new information concerning any of the factors (i.e., the seriousness of the crime, the strength of the evidence and the defendant's social background) pertinent to determining the value of a case. This strategy appears to be consistent with the narrative structure Maynard (1988) found to characterize misdemeanor plea bargaining. However, 'negotiating the value of a case' is perhaps best viewed as the largely tacit, *general* principle (or strategy) that underlies discourse. This principle is illustrated in the following elaborations:

> Kathy: I go in [to the judge's chambers] and say [to the prosecutor] 'What's the offer on this case, Rick?' He tells me, and I usually respond 'Geez Rick! You can give me something better than that!' And give the D.A. information about the client, information about the case – mitigating factors in essence. [Interviewer: For example?] The client has no record. The client is young. Actually, to be quite truthful, the client's white. [Interviewer: Actually?!] I do indeed. If I've got a young blonde kid out there, you think I'm not gonna tell the D.A. that I've got a young blonde kid out there? You better believe I do! [Interviewer: Wow!] I tell the D.A. 'This kid's really middle-class'. Or 'This man's worked all his life and now after 20 years this whatever, this embezzlement happened'. Or y'know, 'This woman was going through medical problems'. [or] 'There was spousal abuse'.

> Mindy: [Interviewer: What is your typical case like in the disposition department?] I go to the dispo department, you

> wait your turn, you go in and talk to the D.A. and the judge
> the same time. The D.A. makes you an offer. And I do
> different things: If I want my client to take the offer, I think
> he's got a lousy case and he's not gonna be able to win,
> sometimes what I'll do is I'll puff [i.e., inflate the value of]
> my case. You say, 'Hey, these are the weaknesses in your
> case, and I think I could win at trial and this is the reason
> why'. Or, 'This is a lousy search issue, and I'm gonna get the
> evidence suppressed. Give me some reason not to do the
> suppression motion' – which in the back of my mind I'm
> saying there's no way I'm ever gonna win this case. But you
> kind of puff it, and then maybe the D.A. will come down a
> little bit ... Sometimes I'll do things like 'Hey, my guy's got
> a great military record', or sometimes I'll do my sentencing
> stuff. I'll say, 'Hey, look at this Medal of Honor he has.
> Look at this and that'. ... Sometimes they'll buy into it and
> say, 'Yeah you're right, this isn't your average schlock'.

As suggested most especially by Kathy's comments, it is in negotiating the
terms of plea bargains that defendants' class-related characteristics and
lifestyles can most clearly be seen to influence case settlement. Specifically,
in explicit negotiations, the more Defenders are able to bring to bear qualities
of their clients which are consistent with traditional commonsense virtues (i.e.,
virtues assumed to be esteemed by typical judging authorities), the more
equipped they are to negotiate better terms. This means, of course, that
indigent defendants are less able than others to furnish their attorneys with
compelling cultural rhetoric for negotiations. Nevertheless, it is also
important to realize that certain less-than-desirable attributes may also be
minimized, ignored or even overlooked throughout settlement negotiations.
Thus, a defendant's employment status, credentials, physical appearance,
demeanor, level of articulateness or other class characteristics need not be
viewed, reviewed or scrutinized by any of the court actors when adjudicating
the terms of a plea bargain.[13]

As apparent in the last attorney's comments, the Defenders also attempt to
coerce D.A.s and judges into making more acceptable offers by insinuating
that they might proceed further with a case. This is clear in two other
Defenders' comments:

> Robert: Generally speaking, [in plea bargaining] you try and
> point out certain advantages that you may have in a case,

exploit whatever leverage you have. [For example,] 'It's in everybody's best interest to get this thing over with and couldn't they do a little better for a defendant?' Hope that the judge is listening while you're talking.

LuAnn: [Interviewer: How does the offer change?] Well, the D.A. will try to get you to plead to something worse if they have you by the balls. [And then I say,] 'We can win this case, your Honor. Why should we even plead this case out?' [or] 'So, okay, if you want to clutter up the courts with cases, that's fine. Make me an offer that I won't go to trial'.

It should be noted here that the Defenders' use of veiled threats to proceed further as a bargaining tactic presupposes the understanding that court actors prefer plea bargaining to other types of litigation procedures. One explanation frequently offered for this apparent preference is 'case pressure'. Specifically, either the overwhelming number of cases that the criminal court handles is said to precipitate plea bargaining or (conversely) plea bargaining is said to alleviate such case pressure.[14]

While most Defenders indicated that judges and D.A.s experience a great deal of case pressure to plea bargain, only one Defender admitted to feeling any such pressure himself. Consistent with studies that argue other, more ethical factors take precedence in decisions to plea bargain,[15] the remaining Defenders maintained that the primary reason they plea bargain cases is simply because it is in the client's best interest. As two Defenders explained,

Nora: [Interviewer: Why not take every case to trial?] Because most people are guilty. And it's overwhelmingly evident. And a lot of defendants just want out as fast as possible ... The courts couldn't accommodate them all either. [Interviewer: Are you limited by your resources here?] We can get as much resources as we need. If we had more cases going to trial, we could get more resources. The county would have to pay for it if we went to trial. It's just that they don't have the courtrooms and the judges to accommodate it ... That's why the D.A.s office pleads as well as overcharges.

Mindy: [Interviewer: Why not take every case to trial?] Because its not in the client's best interests. [Interviewer: Why not?] Because if the defendant has no good case and he's gonna be found guilty, and – say he's charged with a whole bunch of forgery counts, and he's got ten counts, and he's gonna be found guilty of all of them, and the D.A. says instead of taking this case to trial, I'll give you one count. Obviously it's better to have him plead guilty to one count and have the others dismissed than to go down on all counts ... [In addition,] not that many are going to go to trial because the District Attorney can't try everything. And they have an incentive to offer you something because they can't try everything.

In spite of the facts that they handled the largest percentage of criminal cases in the jurisdiction and that they believed judges and D.A.s experienced a great deal of case pressure to plea bargain cases, never did the Defenders threaten D.A.s or judges with the peril of taking *all* their cases to trial. This may have been because, unlike the public Defenders studied by Skolnick (1967) and McDonald (1985), their caseload was relatively small and they consequently had less resources and power to muster (Utz, 1978). Nevertheless, they did employ the threat of proceeding further *with individual cases* to increase their leverage during informal negotiations.

When the Defenders are unable to negotiate acceptable settlement terms through the techniques described above, they *actually* proceed further with a case. In the next scheduled hearing, they then attempt again to negotiate informally a more acceptable offer prior to the formal proceeding. If unsuccessful, they attempt to negotiate an acceptable offer *during* the formal litigation proceeding.

Plea bargain negotiations conducted during litigation proceedings intended for other purposes actually parallel the adversarial proceedings that ordinarily occur in these hearings. However, the Defenders keep in mind the goal of achieving an acceptable plea bargain. Consequently, they frequently put forth information in these hearings that affects the value of a case but may not be entirely relevant to the formal issue at hand (e.g., they present sentencing information at a preliminary hearing).[16] They also continue to solicit informally an incentive to settle. Two Defenders revealed this negotiation strategy in the following comments:

Tom: [S]ometimes I will look at a case and say, 'This is a case which I want to settle', and I will be pushing for settlement [throughout] the entire [litigation process]. I will try to put enough equitable information before the judge

during prelim just so the D.A. gets the idea. I will file
motions in Superior Court sometimes ... knowing that the
purpose of that motion is two-fold: Trying to get the charge
dismissed – which is probably unlikely given the way the
[law] is interpreted, and to ... educate the deputy [i.e.,
Assistant District Attorney] on the upper level [i.e., in
superior court] that he's dealing with a shitty case ... And
sometimes I'll get better offers.

William: I will research [search and seizure issues] for the
preliminary hearing with the hopes that I can beat the D.A.'s
case or at least parts of it. Again, *that will effect the value of
the case as it goes through the system* ... [During preliminary
hearings, I will] try to undermine the D.A.'s case as much as
I can. Try to nip and tuck any evidence that I can. Try to get
rid of it. Try to show the D.A. that his witnesses have
problems. Try to set the scene for my theory of the defense
later on, and at the same time, try to make that transcript
stand out [with problems] so my plea bargain later will be the
best one that I can get. [Emphasis added.]

As the above discussion indicates, important issues in plea bargaining
emerge during litigation proceedings formally intended for other purposes.
This suggests a reciprocal relationship between plea bargaining and other
pretrial and trial proceedings. It also lends credence to Neubauer's (1974)
depiction of plea bargaining as a 'mini-trial' and Maynard's suggestion that
plea bargain negotiations 'are rehearsals of scenes that participants would be
willing to portray before a jury (1984b: 114)'. Perhaps most importantly, it
makes the distinctions between plea bargaining and trial seem less significant.
The latter in particular is apparent in Kathy's discussion on how she handles
settlement cases differently from trial cases. Although she states clearly in this
discussion that *some* type of distinct difference exists in the way she handles
the different types of cases, it is not entirely obvious even to her what that
difference always is. Upon final analysis, it would appear that the difference
is related to the differing strengths of evidence in the cases – a difference
which influences the Defender's original opinion of whether a case is triable
in the first place!

Kathy: I think basically for an experienced attorney, you basically know what kind of case you've got when you see it. You say this is a negotiation case, this case is gonna cop out. And some cases you look at them, and after you interview the client, you know this case is gonna be tried. Those cases you know are on a trial track, I handle differently. Other cases, you basically go through the same steps, but for a different reason. A case that's on a trial track, you'll do a different kind of investigation. The other cases, basically you're planning the sentencing from the day you get the case because you know the guy's gonna cop out. Trial track cases you're not looking so much *just for* mitigating sentencing issues [but instead are] thoroughly investigating the facts of the case. *Now you do that with the other cases too*, but for some reason – basically the evidence of the case and a clear showing of guilt on part of the defendant – you realize that this is not a case that can be tried. But trial track cases, you do a much more involved investigation [and] you do the prelim differently. I do extensive prelims on trial track cases. I subpoena witnesses which I do not ordinarily do – although I have been subpoenaing witnesses in to get sentencing issues in on the preliminary transcript so that they're on the record. That's a new technique – I don't do it real often, but sometimes I do. If it's a complicated case or a very serious case, then I will call witnesses in for the prelim just for purposes of mitigating circumstances. But the trial track cases, you're doing comprehensive preliminary hearings to find out what the witnesses are gonna say. *You also sometimes do that on negotiating cases* so that the D.A. will know the problems with the case – putting people on notice. [Emphasis added.]

To what extent the Defender actually proceeds further with a case depends on when or whether he or she receives an acceptable offer for a guilty plea. What role the defendant plays in this decision-making is discussed below.

Counseling the Defendant and Deciding on a Course of Action

Upon developing a professional opinion of an offer for a guilty plea, the Defenders proceed to advise their clients. Their primary goals in this interaction are to educate (or counsel) the defendant concerning what he or she can reasonably expect in the case and to ascertain the defendant's desires. *Never* do Defenders insist that their clients accept or reject an offer for a guilty plea, and any final decision to plea bargain or take a case to trial *always* rests with the client.

For the most part, the Defender's stance while counseling defendants appears to be consistent with what Flemming (1986) found to be typical of other defense attorneys who represent public clients. Specifically, Flemming found that in order to win their clients' confidence as well as avoid allegations of professional incompetence, attorneys who represent public clients play an advisory rather than a stronger, more insistent recommendatory role. This actually results in public clients' greater involvement in the development of their cases.

Similarly, the Defenders are careful never to dictate to their clients, never to assume they have complete control over their clients' cases, and never to assume that their clients trust them.[17] Indeed! Their approach may be best described as conciliatory. This is apparent in Ingmar's discussion of how he counsels defendants. In this discussion, it appears that Ingmar seeks not merely to instill trust and confidence in him among his clients but moreover to circumvent any possible claim of unethical conduct. He does this by meticulously if not too eagerly asserting through conversational techniques his role, their rights and the status of their cases. In particular, he is especially careful not to suggest plea bargaining too strongly.

> I don't have a set function, but I don't say, 'Did you do it?' I do say, 'What happened? What do you know about all this? They say you did it. And they charged you with such and such. What do you know about it?' Before that, I preface it with a lot of stuff. I make sure that he understands his rights and that he understands what my place is – why I'm there ... in terms of that I'm here, I'm on your side, I'm your advocate, what I'm gonna do, what I see my role as, that everything he tells me is confidential and that it's best if he tells me everything he knows about the case ... Some cases where you see that it's not gonna do this guy any good to plead out, you don't want necessarily to hear that he's guilty

– unless he's ready to tell you. You don't want to – you're not the prosecutor. You've got to have a good relationship with this guy. And you don't want to come on strong and say 'I want to know if you're guilty or not guilty' because he's gonna think 'Well, you're supposed to defend me whether I'm guilty or not guilty, and if you're asking me that question right away, you're just a prosecutor. You're just gonna dump me'. That's what they're gonna think, so you don't want to come on that way. You say, 'Tell me what you know'. And maybe later in the case you say, 'Look. I've got this, that, and the other thing, and you say this, and nothing makes sense. All the evidence that comes up points to such and such. I think *maybe* you should be taking the deal. And if you are guilty, you're *probably* better off to admit it right now. Here's why'. ... [I explain to defendants my] evaluation of the case, and what all the possible things that could happen to him are. What the sentence ranges are. What I would expect that he would get within a range – usually. There's no guarantee. And what I think he should do. Then I ask him what he thinks and what questions he has. [Emphasis added]

While the Defenders are careful to maintain an advisory stance toward their clients, they frequently find themselves confronted with clients who have slightly different agendas and are especially resistant to their advice. In these cases, the Defenders behave similarly to the divorce attorneys studied by Sarat and Felstiner (1986). Specifically, the Defenders employ discourse as well as other strategies that conduce to the choices they deem appropriate. As acknowledged by two Defenders:

Janet: [Interviewer: How do you counsel the defendant regarding the offer?] Well I usually tell them 'Look. This is the offer. And this is a good offer or this is a bad offer. It's your choice whether you plead guilty or not'. That's – there's certain things that only the defendant decides. One of them is whether or not to plead guilty ... Sometimes you have to put it stronger than that because the guy may be looking at ten more years if he goes on. He's got all these priors – prior convictions that are gonna [come in] later on. So you say, 'You know, these priors are gonna come in against you if you testify. And if you're convicted, it's gonna make this burglary sixteen years instead of six. So they're offering you six now so maybe you should seriously think about it'.

Steve: The people in custody are the ones that have a lot of run-ins with the law. [Sometimes] they think you're a public Defender and you're gonna try to force them into taking a quick deal ... You have a different attitude with them. Your gesture, your approach to them in your attitude – not in what you *do* for them, but in how you explain what their options are. Sometimes using reverse psychology if you think a person should take the deal ... You explain the reality of the situation as I just did to you, and you say 'but I'm ready to go to trial'. Once they realize you're not resisting their demand to go to trial and their demand that they pay you some attention, and you indicate to them by whatever way that you'll take their case to trial and that's why you're doing this type of work – because you like to do trial work and that's more fun than filling out a change of plea form, then they will drop their resistance to a plea bargain based specifically on you as the dump truck who doesn't care about them.

As outlined in Table 1, there are five possible combinations of Defender-client input that result in one of two actual outcomes to a plea bargaining episode. The following discussion provides rough estimates of their prevalence and describes at least some of their essential ingredients.

Table 1. Types of Defender-client Input and Outcomes to Plea Bargaining Episodes

Defender's Recommendation	Client's Desire	Actual Outcome
Plead	Plead	Settlement
Proceed further	Plead	Settlement
Plead	Different terms	Settlement or Proceed further
Plead	Trial	Proceed further
Proceed further	Proceed further	Proceed further

Both Defender and Client Agree on Plea Bargain The easiest and probably most frequent mode of interaction is when the Defender establishes that the defendant should accept an offer and the defendant agrees. In these instances, the case is settled immediately.

A case that illustrates this type is one that involved a male defendant charged with burglary and providing false identification to a police officer. The defendant was apprehended inside the bathroom of a restaurant while two other co-defendants were caught outside the building. The only things found missing were donuts. The defendant wanted to take full responsibility for the crimes, but the Defender told him that a plea bargain meant that all three defendants would have to admit some sort of guilt. The Defender also stated that all the defendants *could* be sent to prison for burglary if found guilty by a jury. All three defendants ultimately decided they would plea bargain to second-degree burglary as a misdemeanor – the standard offer. I helped the defendant complete a plea agreement form while the Defender negotiated the terms with the D.A. The defendants were then sentenced the same day.

Defender Recommends Proceeding Further and Client Desires Plea Bargain Another frequent mode of interaction is when the Defender recommends proceeding further with a case and the defendant desires to plea bargain. As Feeley (1977) has found, many defendants are not interested in taking their cases to trial because it entails costs which otherwise would not be incurred. For the Defenders' clients, these costs are typically believed to be increased jail time. As stated by two Defenders:

> Karl: Sometimes – it's usually me coming to [defendants] with an offer. [However,] There are many clients that realize that they are in a very bad situation factually – versus the prosecution. And they bring up plea bargaining. I had a client bring up plea-bargaining to me just yesterday wanted to know what kind of deal we could get real quick. [Interviewer: What was he interested in?] He was interested in getting out of jail.

> Nora: [Interviewer: Why not take every case to trial?] ... [A] lot of defendants just want out [of jail] as fast as possible. They don't want to stay in as long as possible. They want out faster. They want to get rid of it, be done with it, serve the time, and get out.

One case that illustrates this type of interaction involved a defendant charged with commercial burglary. The Defender believed the defendant had a triable case because (arguably) the alleged victim had actually reneged on a business deal in which he had agreed to sell some merchandise for the defendant. The Defender believed he could assert that the defendant was merely attempting to regain charge over his own merchandise. However, the defendant did not want a trial because he feared public humiliation and because he wanted to go home to another state. Consequently, the case was settled immediately.

In another case of commercial burglary, however, the defendant insisted that all he wanted was to get out of jail and go home (again, to another state) as soon as possible. Although this case was eventually dismissed, the prosecutor later refiled the charges when more evidence and a rather serious prior record were discovered. Thus, in retrospect, it appeared that this defendant's desire to dispose of the case as quickly as possible was actually motivated by the desire to avoid more serious penalties.

Regardless of the defendant's actual reasons for desiring to plea bargain, in cases where the defendant wants to plea bargain in spite of the Defender's advice to proceed further, the case is settled immediately.

Defender Recommends Plea Bargain and Client Desires Different Terms
If not the most typical, another very frequent mode of interaction is when the Defender recommends a plea bargain but the defendant prefers plea agreement terms other than those initially offered. When this occurs, the Defenders usually engage in explicit negotiations in order to make a guilty plea acceptable.

A case characteristic of this type involved a defendant who was initially charged with using force and inflicting injury upon a police officer and obstructing a public officer in the discharge of his duty. The defendant was offered a felony that would be reduced to a misdemeanor after a year's successful probation and up to one year in jail. The defendant bemoaned having a felony on his record and worried about losing his job by spending time in jail. The Defender in this case returned to the judge's chambers and reported that the defendant did not want the deal. He argued that the defendant did not *intend* to harm anyone (the prosecutor was responsible for proving intent). The judge then intervened by promising to give the defendant a misdemeanor at sentencing if he paid restitution beforehand. (The Defender later informed me that he knew the defendant would also get work furlough because 'this judge would not want the defendant to lose his job'.)

If a Defender is unsuccessful in negotiating more acceptable plea bargain terms in these cases, the defendant then decides whether to accept the offer for a guilty plea anyway (which frequently occurs) or to 'proceed further' with the case (which usually occurs because the Defender concludes that a different D.A. or judge will be more amenable). If the latter occurs, another decision-making process occurs again later on and another episode of plea-bargaining transpires. If an acceptable offer is ever made to the defendant, a plea bargain agreement proceeds to be finalized. Otherwise, the attorney could engage in *rounds* of plea-bargaining[18] and ultimately litigate the case completely in front of a jury.

Defender Recommends Plea Bargain and Client Desires Trial   When counseled about the small chance they have of winning their cases, some defendants *insist* not merely that they are innocent but also on taking their cases to trial. Among those cases which the researcher observed taken to trial, this type of case appeared to be the most frequent. These defendants fall into that category described by Sudnow (1965) and Neubauer (1974) as 'stubborn'.

These cases typically proceed further down the litigation path toward trial. However, as the case proceeds, the Defenders remain open to and may actively pursue offers for guilty pleas. They also continue to advise their clients about the virtues of plea bargaining. If an acceptable offer is ever made to the defendant, the case proceeds to be settled. This usually occurs when the defendant concedes that he or she could suffer more severe consequences by being found guilty through trial.

One case that illustrates this mode involved a defendant charged with three counts of burglary. The defendant insisted that he was innocent in spite of his previous confession and other very incriminating evidence against him. Convinced that the defendant would be seriously hurt through trial, the Defender went directly into the judge's chambers immediately prior to the preliminary hearing in order to negotiate a plea bargain. The Defender then met with the defendant and told him the offer (i.e., one count of aiding and abetting credit card forgery, reduced to a misdemeanor in eighteen months).

Although the defendant in this case continued to resist plea bargaining initially, the Defender reiterated the strong evidence against him and the possible penalties associated with a plea bargain versus a trial. Eventually, the defendant requested and accepted slightly revised settlement terms (i.e., 'receiving stolen property' instead of 'aiding and abetting credit card forgery').

If a defendant in this type of case is never convinced that plea bargaining is desirable, the Defender engages in rounds of plea bargaining episodes and the case is completely litigated in front of a jury. And although the researcher never actually witnessed such an instance, several horror stories were related to her about defendants who got seriously hurt after trial because they refused to plea bargain.

Defender Recommends Proceeding Further and Client Desires to Proceed Further A final mode of interaction occurs when the Defender advises the defendant to proceed further with the case and the defendant agrees. This usually occurs because the D.A. does not make the defendant a 'reasonable' offer for a guilty plea.[19] This appeared to be the second most likely type of case to go to trial.[20] Like the former type, the Defenders in these cases remain open to and may actively pursue guilty plea offers. If an acceptable offer is ever made to the defendant, the case is settled. Otherwise, these cases may be completely litigated in front of a jury.

One example of this type of case involved a defendant accused of two counts of assault with a deadly weapon, one count of brandishing a weapon against a police officer, and one count of being under the influence of PCP. According to the Defender, the D.A. would not offer the defendant anything due to the seriousness of the crime and the defendant's prior record. On the day of the preliminary hearing, the D.A. asked that the case be 'trailed' (a shorter and more tentative delay than a continuance) because two of her witnesses had not shown up. Fearing that a dismissal would result simply in the case being refiled again later, the Defender seized the opportunity to pursue a plea bargain. To the Defender's dismay, the D.A. refused to deal and the two missing witnesses showed up while other witnesses were testifying. The case did ultimately plead out, however, when the formerly missing witnesses became reluctant to testify against the defendant, who was one's brother and the other's friend.

A final comment should be added here regarding interaction in which the Defender advises an agreeable client to take a case to trial because the case is actually triable. This is the rarest mode of interaction and is frequently assumed by outside observers to bypass plea-bargaining altogether. However, it was found in this study that these cases rarely proceed to trial completion because the D.A. either drops the charges against the defendant or offers the defendant 'a very good deal'.[21] Consequently, even when the Defenders advise their clients to take their cases to trial and they agree, it is perhaps better viewed as simply another instance of 'proceeding further'.

A Note on Accepting the Plea Bargain When a defendant has accepted the terms of a plea bargain, a plea agreement proceeds to be finalized. In becoming finalized, a contract is first drawn. This contract states not only the specific terms of the agreement, but also what rights and responsibilities are assigned to which party in the agreement.

After the contract is drawn, the Defender reviews with the defendant the terms of the agreement. The defendant then initials the contract alongside each critical stipulation as an indication of his or her understanding. The defendant, the Defender, and the prosecuting attorney then sign the contract.

After the contract is signed and initialed, it is officially and publicly confirmed in open court. The confirmation consists of the judge reading, getting a factual basis for, and reviewing aloud the plea bargain contract with the defendant in the presence of both attorneys. A court reporter records the verbal interaction for official record. A sentencing hearing is then slated for the defendant at the end of the hearing.

Conclusion

For Defenders, plea bargaining may include multiple episodes of negotiating behavior as well as a wide range of litigation proceedings. Most importantly, plea-bargaining and trial can actually be seen to converge: not only are settlement negotiations 'rehearsals of scenes that participants would be willing to portray before a jury' (Maynard, 1984b:114), but also pretrial and trial proceedings are oftentimes precursors for case settlement. In addition, the manner in which Defenders plea bargain provides defendants with a great deal of latitude in deciding their own fates; i.e., not only is their right to due-process preserved but they are at the same time provided with the opportunity to limit what may be unwarranted penalties.[22] Thus, Defenders do not merely represent their clients effectively through plea bargaining, but perhaps afford them greater justice through case settlement than through trial.

Regardless, poor criminal suspects can still be seen to incur some injustice in plea bargaining. Namely, even though indigent defendants are subject to less public scrutiny and their attorneys are therefore better able to limit the impact of discrediting yet innocuous and therefore irrelevant cultural information about them, their lower-class lifestyles and characteristics nonetheless debilitate the rhetoric that Defenders are able to employ on their behalf throughout plea negotiations. Consequently, poor defendants are more likely than others to be convicted of crimes as well as convicted of serious crimes *regardless of* their actual innocence or guilt.[23]

Notes

1   This is important to consider when attempting to reconcile Myers' (1980) findings with those presented in this chapter. According to Myers, such attributes as a defendant's age, sex, and employment status do not differently effect the sanctions defendants receive after being convicted by trial as compared to plea-bargaining. However, in studying the relationship between defendants' sentences and mode of disposition, Myers does not consider that a defendant's attributes may effect the sentence he receives by *first* affecting the number or the seriousness of the crimes for which they are convicted. In other words, Myers' study appears to presuppose sentence bargaining rather than charge bargaining. More will be said about these studies in a later footnote.

2   See also Maynard (1988) Ryan and Alfini (1979).

3   See also Skolnick (1967). It should also be noted that on those rare occasions when a judge rejects a plea bargain agreed upon by the prosecutor and the Defender, the two attorneys generally take the case before another judge who presides over court hearings further along in the adjudication process (see also Utz, 1978). Rarely if ever do the Defenders challenge judges for plea bargaining issues. This is because attorneys are allowed only one preemptory challenge to a judge per case and the Defenders usually want to save that challenge in case they are forced to take the case to trial in front of an unfavorable trial judge.

4   In discussing misdemeanor plea-bargaining, Maynard states, 'For each case, the defense and prosecution must determine some disposition (which may be anything from a dismissal to a jail sentence), or must agree to a trial date, or must agree to continue the case for reconsideration at a later time (1984b: 78)'. The concept of 'proceeding further' differs in that it is a less formal outcome of a plea bargaining episode and does not specifically mean that a case will be scheduled for trial or that another settlement hearing will be scheduled. (All the Defenders' cases have tentative trial dates when they are received and serious felonies have two settlement hearings scheduled automatically.) Instead, it means that a case will simply proceed to whatever formal proceeding it ordinarily would if the actual intention was to take it to trial.

5   In contrast, most researchers have examined plea-bargaining in a manner that suggests it involves only a single episode of negotiating behavior. See for example, Albonetti (1992), Alschuler (1975), Blumberg (1967a, 1967b), Church (1976), Eisenstein and Jacob (1977), Eisenstein, Flemming, and Nardulli (1988), Farr (1984), Feeley (1977), McConville and Mirsky (1990), McDonald (1985), Mileski (1971), Rosett and Cressey (1976), Skolnick (1967), Sudnow (1965) and Uhlman and Walker (1979).

6   The American Bar Association (1986) considers it the defense attorney's ethical obligation both to convey offers for guilty pleas to their clients and to accept them on their behalf when their clients desire to settle a case. Conversely, they are not legally permitted to accept such offers without their clients' permission.

7   See also Feeley (1977), Mather (1979), McDonald (1985), Neubauer (1974) and Rosett and Cressey (1976).

8   See also Feeley (1977), Mather (1979), McDonald (1985) and Neubauer (1974).

9   See also McDonald (1985) and Utz (1978).

10 As discussed below, this may also be the case among the attorneys studied by Maynard (1984a; 1984b; 1988).

11 Similar findings are reported by Eisenstein et al (1988), Maynard (1984a; 1984b; 1988) and McDonald (1979).

12 See also Maynard (1984a: 108).

13 It is important to note here once again, that Myers (1980) found that such attributes as a
defendant's age, sex, and employment status do not differently effect the sanctions
defendants receive after being convicted by trial as compared to plea bargaining. Based on
this, Myers further concludes that a defendant's presence during a trial makes little or no
difference on sentencing. However, not only may Myers have mistakenly assumed that
sentence bargaining (rather than charge bargaining) was occurring (and therefore defendants
who plea bargained received less severe sentences *due to reduced charges*), but due to this
possible omission, she was also unable to consider whether lower-status defendants
benefited further in these reductions because they were less apt to influence negatively the
narrative told on their behalf during plea bargaining.

14 See, for example, Alschuler (1968), Blumberg (1967a), Church (1976), Holmes et al (1987),
Kingsnorth and Jungsten (1988), Padgett (1990) and Utz (1978).

15 See, for example, Feeley (1973; 1977), Heumann (1975; 1979), McDonald (1985) and
Skolnick (1967).

16 It is important to distinguish this type of plea bargaining technique from that of the 'slow
plea' described by Mather (1979). In 'slow pleas', the judge, prosecutor and defense
attorney involved in the case predetermine the outcome of the court hearing. This does not
occur when the Defenders 'proceed further' with a case and subterraneously attempt to
negotiate plea bargains throughout other types of court hearings.

17 Skolnick (1967) also argued that public clients were more difficult for attorneys to control.

18 Maynard (1984b: 101) makes this observation about the attorneys he studied. The primary
difference here is that rounds of negotiation occur not because the attorneys have continued
a settlement hearing but because the Defenders continue to solicit offers and negotiate plea
bargains as a case proceeds further.

19 Utz (1978) also found this in her study. It should also be noted that this mode of decision-
making also includes cases in which the D.A. refuses to plea bargain. In these instances, the
defendant does not have any choice but to take the case to trial.
Another relevant observation that should be made here concerns the more serious sentences
that defendants receive after convictions at trials than for the same offenses after plea-
bargaining. Although LaFree (1985) and Uhlman and Walker (1979; 1980) found that
defendants who plea bargain generally receive less severe sentences than those who are
convicted after trial, the findings reported in this study suggest that perhaps the latter
defendants sometimes receive more severe sentences, not as punishment for taking their
case to trial, but because the defense attorneys were for some reason unsuccessful in
negotiating more acceptable offers.

20 This is somewhat supported by Harris and Springer's (1984) finding that attorneys who
represent clients with serious prior records will be more likely to go to trial than to plea
bargain. Their finding may reflect the fact that prosecutors offer defendants whose cases
have little value only little incentive to plea bargain. Consequently, these defendants have
little or nothing to lose by taking their case to trial.

21 See also Farr (1984: 311).

22 It is important to note here McConville's (1986) contention that trials do not guarantee that
truth will prevail. Insofar as adversarial procedures do not guarantee that the guilty will be
convicted or the innocent set free, and because our judicial system espouses that defendants
should be given the benefit of doubt (i.e., assumed innocent until proven guilty), it seems
this type of plea bargaining system can ensure justice as much or more than trials.

23 The findings of Holmes et al (1987) might also be seen as inconsistent with those reported
here. According to these researchers, social status has only little direct effect on charge

reductions in plea bargaining, and this effect is not in the expected direction. Instead, minority defendants tend to receive less severe responses. While the authors suggest an explanation for this discrepancy (i.e., some initial overcharging by the prosecutor), it is pertinent to add here that my findings suggest some additional reasons. First, since the effect of social status on plea bargaining is less than what it is in a trial, one would expect commensurately less association between plea bargain reductions and social status. Second, as discussed in Chapter Three, my findings indicate that social status should also be seen to play a role in plea bargaining through a defendant's prior offense record. This is a variable for which Holmes et al have controlled in their study, however.

Chapter Six

Conclusion

[T]he claims justice makes on law are powerful, yet the
vindication of justice through law is by no means certain.
Only by attending to context, history, and contingency can we
understand, most often in retrospect, why, on this occasion or
that, law was the ally of injustice and the adversary of justice.
Only by suspending the rituals of philosophical abstraction
can scholars identify the conditions under which law heeds
the call of justice. Only by doing so can scholarship help
promote a more just legality (Austin Sarat and Thomas
Kearns, 1998a: 17).

This book has been a study of justice for the poor. It has considered whether
poor criminal suspects are fairly represented through the everyday defense
work of one group of publicly provided attorneys. Overall, the study has
produced two major findings. First, contrary to popular opinion and the
conclusions drawn by numerous researchers regarding lawyers for the poor,[1]
the Defenders maintain an adversarial stance toward the prosecuting attorney
and seek to protect their clients' interests to the fullest extent prescribed by law.
In this sense, their behavior can be characterized as legally ethical, or, because
it implies compliance with formally prescribed legal procedures, 'procedurally
just'.[2] Second, despite their legally ethical representation, social class
nonetheless unduly shapes the manner by which Defenders advocate on behalf
of poor suspects. Thus, because law is invoked on the basis of inequitable
social conditions, indigent defendants can be characterized as the victims of
'substantive injustice'.[3]

Procedural Justice for the Poor: A Focus on their Legal Advocates

The problem of justice for poor criminal suspects is typically conceived as one
of inadequate legal representation. This study finds that although Defenders are
unable to handle every criminal case as if they have unlimited time and
resources (a situation which might be possible if they worked solely for wealthy

clients), it is simply incorrect to suggest that they do not represent their clients ethically.

As discussed in Chapter Two, an adversarial stance among Defenders is initially cultivated through the role prerequisite behaviors of key court actors. Even if only minimally, the very purpose for the existence of prosecutors, defense attorneys, judges, juries, witnesses and defendants presupposes that some type of opposing interests underlies the interaction which takes place among them. An adversarial stance is further cultivated through the legal professionals' macro-referenced behaviors. That is, empowered through and largely motivated by their desire to safeguard Constitutional edicts, Defenders battle judges and prosecutors who they believe bring to bear the dictates and potential tyranny of the powerful. Thus, as McIntyre (1987) finds, not only does an adversarial character appear to be cultivated by the court system's need to maintain legitimacy but this situation implies a contradiction whereby a truly effective public Defender system entails calling into question the legitimacy of behaviors performed by other members of the court system.

The battles in which the Defenders engage are story-telling battles. The parameters and 'weapons' for these battles are prescribed and circumscribed by the cultural domains of common sense and legal expertise, language or symbolic systems that comprise what Kenneth Burke (1989) would call the 'grammar' and 'rhetoric' of the legal professionals' social action.[4]

Chapters Three, Four, and Five described precisely how the Defenders choose, prepare for and engage in their legal battles. In Chapter Three, we examined how Defenders develop a professional opinion regarding the best mode of case disposition; i.e., either a jury trial or a plea bargain. In Chapter Four, we examined how these attorneys prepare for and litigate trials. We considered how Defenders negotiate the terms of case settlements in Chapter Five. Overall, Defenders could be seen to represent their clients ethically and accord them procedural justice in the following ways:

- The strength of evidence is a critical consideration in their assessments of whether a case should be plea bargained or taken to trial. Thus, keeping the D.A. accountable and whether the defendant could actually be convicted legally of crime are important issues to Defenders.[5]

- The Defenders' motive for considering whether a case should be plea bargained or taken to trial is to determine whether the defendant might incur less cost (or legal penalty) through one mode of disposition versus the other.[6] This means that their goal is to protect their clients' interests and that their allegiance is not to the D.A. or judge but instead to their clients.

- Defenders counsel their clients carefully and are especially scrupulous in ensuring that it is the client who ultimately decides whether a case will be plea bargained or taken to trial.[7] Thus, these indigent defendants are fully apprised of the potential consequences associated with either course of action and are able to invoke or recant their right to due process in a conscientious manner.

- In taking cases to trial, Defenders employ a variety of both expected and somewhat surprising and creative methods of preparation. Thus, trials are carefully prepared and these attorneys take their responsibilities in this task quite seriously.

- In plea bargaining, Defenders routinely attempt not only to 'up' the D.A.'s ante for a guilty plea but also to barter terms tailored to their clients' preferences. In addition and perhaps most importantly, until they have achieved terms that are acceptable to their clients, they continue to litigate the case as if it were going to trial. This means that unless and until their clients become amenable to a settlement, their right to a jury trial is preserved.

Substantive Justice for the Poor: The Influence of Social Class

Although Defenders can be seen to accord their clients procedural justice, this does not mean that their clients encounter *no* injustice in the adjudication of their cases. On the contrary, this study reveals that social class influences a great deal of their attorneys' behavior. However, its influence emerges through the Defenders' expectations of how the judge and jury evaluate the cases of indigent defendants and therefore what constitutes viable defense rhetoric.[8] This can then be seen to affect case outcomes *regardless of* a defendant's actual guilt or innocence of crime.

As discussed in Chapter Two, the role prerequisite behaviors of judges, jurors, witnesses, and defendants bring about a set of relationships whereby some persons are accorded the power to pass judgement onto others. It is through macro-referenced conduct, however, that social class is brought to bear in these relationships: judges and jurors are thought to assess lower-class defendants and other witnesses on the basis of middle-class sensibilities.[9] This class bias is expressed through the different cultural domains of meaning (or language systems) that these court actors employ. In particular, while judges and jurors are expected to uphold a traditional, commonsense value and belief system (or the values, beliefs and norms of the status quo), lower-class defendants and their personal allies tend to employ a culturally disparate system. Thus, poor criminal suspects typically lack the cultural resources (or compelling language) with which to present themselves and be presented as socially acceptable and 'upstanding' members of our society to judging authorities.

The precise manners in which social class influences adjudicative behavior through the grammar and rhetoric of common sense and legal expertise were discussed in Chapters Three, Four and Five. The conclusions drawn therein include the following:

- The more the defendant's characteristics and lifestyle as reflected in evidence stories are consistent with commonsense or status quo values and beliefs, the stronger (or more persuasive) the defense evidence is deemed to be. Because poor defendants' characteristics and lifestyles tend to be at variance with status quo sentiments, they are more likely to have defense evidence that is perceived as weak.

- The more a defendant's characteristics and lifestyle are consistent with commonsense or status quo values and beliefs, the more valuable his case is deemed to be. Because poor defendants' characteristics and lifestyles are more likely to be at variance with status quo sentiments, they are likely to have less valuable cases, be offered less incentive to plea bargain, and have less to lose by taking their cases to trial.

- The defendant's social class affects the Defender's ability to prepare cases for trial. Because their clients are less able to assist with their defenses in general, Defenders are less able to build viable evidence stories and prepare their story-telling strategies.

- Because defendants are not usually present during plea bargain negotiations, certain discrediting information need not and may not be revealed throughout this process. This suggests that plea bargaining may be more substantively just for indigent defendants than trial.

- Nevertheless, the defendant's social class affects the manner by which Defenders negotiate the terms of plea bargains. In explicit plea bargaining, Defenders introduce mitigating information on behalf of their client. In general, the more a defendant's social characteristics and lifestyle are consistent with commonsense or status quo values and standards, the more Defenders are able to invoke mollifying or conciliatory information on his or her behalf (i.e., they are more able to convince others that their client is a 'respectable', largely moral person who does not warrant severe criminal sanctions.) Because poor defendants' social characteristics and lifestyles are more likely to be at variance with status quo values and standards, they are less able to provide their attorneys with effective rhetoric by which to mitigate their cases for plea bargaining purposes.

- As may be apparent from all the above, in litigating their clients' guilt, Defenders are compelled to tell evidence stories in the language of the powerful. Thus only those stories that the powerful are amenable to hearing get told and the plights, storylines and perspectives of the less powerful poor are precluded.

- Overall, although poor criminal suspects have less to lose by taking their cases to trial, they are also more likely to be convicted of crime, acquire a record of prior convictions and receive more severe sentences *regardless of their actual guilt of crime.*

A Note on Commonsense Sexism and Racism in the Adjudication of Criminal Cases

Not surprisingly, this study concludes that poor criminal suspects are more likely to be convicted of crimes, be convicted of more serious crimes and receive more severe sentences than other defendants. What may be surprising is the reason provided for such rates. It is argued that these outcomes occur *not* because the poor are improperly represented by their attorneys or because the poor actually warrant such sanctions, but because circumstances associated with the defendants' social class enter into adjudication procedures and unduly tip the scales of justice against them. This occurs through what might ordinarily appear to be the wholly benign and useful practice of commonsense reasoning.

While commonsense reasoning in the adjudication of criminal cases involves discrimination against the poor, it also entails sexism and racism. Regarding sexism, the use of 'common sense' in criminal court proceedings means that traditional or status quo standards pertaining to men and women underlie these proceedings and produce inequitable outcomes for men and women. Evidence for such a situation can be seen in Daly's (1987) findings regarding court officials' rationale for imposing different sentences on men and women and in Matoesian's (1995) study of the Kennedy Smith rape trial.[10]

According to Daly, judges make distinctions not merely between familied and nonfamilied defendants but between familied men and familied women. Defendants with families receive leniency when more severe penalties would result in suffering on the part of innocent family members. Familied men, however, are treated more leniently when they are employed and supporting a family, and familied women are treated more leniently simply when they have children because the mother's childcare is deemed more important than the economic support they could provide. Herein we can see that the judges in this study made decisions on the basis of traditional (or commonsense) notions regarding men and women's roles in our society, and thereby imposed inequitable sentences on them.

According to Matoesian, defense attorneys in the Kennedy Smith rape trial attempted to impeach the victim (apparently successfully insofar as they won the case) by eliciting information that implied her behavior and background were inconsistent with the stereotype of male/female sexual relations. Like that employed by the judges in Daly's study, this image consisted of traditional (or commonsense) expectations regarding 'appropriate' sexual conduct for men and women in our society. That prosecutors did not attempt to impeach the defendant with some type of similar tactic (i.e., by attempting to establish that his behavior was inconsistent with *some other* ideal of male/female sexual relations) suggests further that the trial stratagems of both types of attorneys were circumscribed by their shared expectations concerning the jury's traditional *or commonsense* understandings of 'appropriate' sexual conduct for men and women.

Both types of the commonsense discrimination described above can be seen to affect some minority groups a great deal more than the dominant group due to a minority group's overrepresentation in poverty rates.[11] However, there are also indications in this study that minority groups encounter some discrimination beyond that based on class and gender. This is revealed in the foregoing analysis by several Defenders' explicit references to race as an important variable in predicting adjudicative outcomes. The data suggests that racial and ethnic minorities encounter additional disadvantages in the adjudication of criminal cases due to cultural practices and experiences which distinguish them from the dominant white group, and which make it more difficult to portray their cases in a manner that complies with the cultural views of the status quo, or, common sense. This appears to occur in two major ways.

First, some discrimination is associated with the use of categories that designate membership in particular racial or ethnic groups. While conceding that their use is sometimes beneficial, these categories nonetheless stereotype people and indicate that some are 'different' from others. When people are perceived as 'different', they are also regarded as somewhat unfamiliar and therefore seem a bit more fearsome and morally suspect than others. Such perceptions is perhaps most apparent in one Defender's (i.e., Kathy's) contention that asserting a defendant is white during plea bargaining has a moderating influence; i.e., this characterization portrays the defendant as a more familiar and appealing person than other types to those in positions of authority.

Second and perhaps most importantly, due to their different experiences of the social order, the dominant group cannot understand or appreciate fully situations of racial oppression in their own society. Enmeshed in their own largely segregated and relatively safe social worlds, for example, most whites in this country cannot actually fathom why contemporary minority groups proclaim discrimination, and find minority experiences of police exploitation especially difficult to believe. Thus, Karl and Betty along with most if not all the other Defenders acknowledge some complications in portraying the cases of their minority clients in a manner that is consistent with the commonsense attitudes held by those adjudicating the cases, which is the same thing as the cultural understandings of the *white* status quo.

Implications Regarding Future Research

Numerous researchers have studied the effects of defendants' social class or status on criminal case outcomes. While many of the findings are consistent with those presented here,[12] others encompass various types and degrees of discrepancy.[13] This study suggests several reasons for the disagreements among research findings as well as possible methods for reconciling them.

First, these findings indicate that it is important for researchers to measure the concept of social class through variables that reflect the perspectives of the key actors involved in assigning meaning and effectuating criminal case outcomes. This is because it is the classifications or gestalt of characteristics that the participants themselves employ and not those of researchers that influence their behavior. Most quantitative studies do not consider members' perspectives and their interpretive categories in measuring social class.[14]

Second, the findings presented here show that social class affects adjudicative outcomes as both extra-legal *as well as legal variables*. As suspected by Farrell (1971) and Swigert and Farrell (1977), social class affects not only the strength of the evidence in criminal cases, but also (by implication) defendants' prior records. However, these are factors for which almost all quantitative researchers control in their studies. Their findings are consequently likely to underestimate *substantially* the effect of social class on criminal case outcomes.[15]

Finally, this study indicates that social class affects the sentences which defendants receive through both their prior criminal records as well as through the method by which they are plea-bargained. In particular, it is important to recognize the distinction between 'charge bargaining' and 'sentence bargaining'. The first means that attorneys negotiate the crime(s) to which defendants plead guilty and the second means that they negotiate the penalty. It appears that many, if not most, prosecutors employ charge bargaining and that the reduced charges then result in lighter sentences. Consequently, it may be unrealistic to consider whether defendants receive harsher sentences for taking their cases to trial by controlling for the crime of which they were convicted or to conclude that because there is no significant difference in the sentences, that the defendant's visibility makes no difference to the outcome of his or her case.[16] Instead, it is quite possible that the defendant's visibility affected *first* the crime for which he or she was convicted and *then* the sentence.

The Problem of Achieving Justice for the Poor: Implications for Social Reform

As suggested above, the problem of achieving justice for poor criminal suspects can be seen to encompass two types of concerns. These are the concerns for achieving procedural justice and substantive justice. While the first emphasizes attorneys' behavior and its conformity with the ideals of due process, the second emphasizes the effects of the larger social context. This section discusses each of these concerns in light of findings produced by this study.

The Problem of Achieving Procedural Justice

For the most part, scholars who express concern for achieving procedural justice suggest that indigent persons are not receiving the same quality of advocacy as non-indigents. Conceptualizing the problem in this manner implies that it is the attorneys' behavior that should somehow be changed, and typically it is the system for defending poor criminal suspects that is thought to require some type of reform.[17]

Although numerous investigators have argued that the behavior of publicly provided defense attorneys has generally been misunderstood and mis-evaluated,[18] the findings presented here as well as elsewhere[19] indicate that Defense Alliance was not only relatively successful in providing procedurally ethical defense services to the poor but also somewhat more successful than other types of indigent defense organizations. As such, it is useful to make comparisons between the different types of defense systems in order to ferret out organizational imperatives that might facilitate or obstruct ethical defense representation for the poor.

As a private, nonprofit corporation of court-appointed defense attorneys, Defense Alliance was rather unique among systems for indigent defense. First, as a *privately-run* agency, Defense Alliance operated under the guidance of a relatively independent Board of Trustees. This Board was initially comprised entirely of members of the County Bar Association. As such, it not only maintained a professional stake and interest in the provision of high quality indigent defense service, but also acted as a kind of bulwark against political caprice.[20] This contrasts with the extreme political sensitivity apparently experienced by and channeled through the Public Defenders' Offices studied by Platt and Pollock (1974) and Feeley (1979).

Second, as a type of *corporation*, Defense Alliance was also able to maintain a degree of efficiency greater than that maintained by public bureaucracies. This means that, as Powell[21] noted with regard to other types of private law firms, Defense Alliance was relatively free to engage in types of entrepreneurial activities that promoted its interests. It was able, for example, to take advantage of a competitive market system both in hiring and firing its employees, in procuring outside services, and in otherwise maintaining a professionally-run law office. This contrasts with the Public Defenders' Offices described by Feeley (1979), Platt and Pollock (1974) and McIntyre (1987).

Third, as a *non-profit organization that provided services to the poor*, Defense Alliance attracted into employment attorneys whose political ideologies, occupational goals, and professional ethics were consistent with the goal of *serving the client's interests*. The attorneys were not only committed to civil rights and liberties, but also committed to protecting (if not advancing) the rights and interests of the poor. This is consistent with Erlanger's (1978) and Katz's (1982) findings regarding other types of legal assistance institutions as well as Platt and Pollack's (1974) findings regarding Public Defenders.

Finally, as a *nonprofit* agency, Defenders were not seeking to maximize profit through the services they provided to their clients, and did not base their advocacy around the size or timely payment of a fee. Instead, they advocated on the basis of what they perceived to be the merits of a case as well as on the basis of their clients' requests. This contrasts with the behavior of the private defense attorneys observed by Blumberg (1967b) and Alschuler (1975) and is consistent with Skolnick's (1967) and Alschuler's (1975) observation of Public Defenders.

Overall then, Defense Alliance's success can be attributed to its structure *as* a private, non-profit corporation for the defense of indigent persons. Thus, this type of structure might be utilized to enhance the quality of criminal defense services provided to poor persons everywhere. However, it is also critical to point out here that despite the fact that Defense Alliance had a remarkable record and reputation of providing ethical defense services to indigent persons, its contract with the county was ultimately not renewed at the very point that it was about to assume control over virtually the entire caseload of indigent criminal cases in Smith County. While the precise reasons for the cancellation might be debated among the various factions,[22] I believe the actual reason was because this very successful defense system was too threatening to the legitimacy of other court actors' behaviors. As McIntyre states,

> [B]ecause it is the defense attorney's job to pinpoint the
> mistake of others (police, prosecutors, and even judges),
> competent defense attorneys pose a threat to the legitimacy of
> any criminal justice system that is less than infallible. In view
> of the complexity of its institutional role, the public
> Defender's office's survival seems to hinge on its ability to
> remain obscure (1987: 174).

Thus, in view of Defense Alliance's well-known successes in Smith County, it seems the only way the County Board of Supervisors could re-establish the court system's legitimacy was to institute a less reputable and arguably less effective public Defender system.

It seems, therefore, that bringing about a truly effective system for defending indigent criminal suspects entails overcoming the contradiction that is institutionalized in our criminal court system. One way we might attempt to accomplish this is by pursuing the policy proposed by Jim Neuhard (1986): *we should extend the right to publicly-provided defense counsel to all persons.*

While Neuhard's proposal might at first seem unfeasible, it is important to keep in mind (as he states) that because most criminal cases involve indigent suspects, the increase in costs for providing this service would be minimal. In addition, in light of numerous studies that indicate publicly provided defense attorneys frequently perform at levels comparable to or higher than private attorneys, it is not far-fetched to believe that because the working and middle classes have fewer resources than the wealthy but not little enough to currently qualify for free defense services, these economic groups would truly benefit from this provision.[23] Finally, by extending the right to free representation to everyone, it is possible that enough public interest in and support for civil rights and liberties might be mustered to counteract the ever-present threat of tyranny from the powerful.

While the reforms described above would help to alleviate the problem of achieving *procedural justice*, they leave intact the problem of *substantive* injustice.

The Problem of Achieving Substantive Justice

The problem of achieving substantive justice emphasizes the role of broader social conditions in legal processes.[24] The 'blame' for injustice is usually placed on social inequality and any remedy must *somehow* deal with the inequitable social conditions that skew justice.

Before proceeding to discuss how social reformers might attempt to remedy substantive injustice, it is important to note here what these findings do *not* imply for social reform. Contrary to some observers' suggestions,[25] this study does not indicate that defendants would benefit by being directly involved in plea bargain negotiations. Instead, although this type of involvement might provide defendants with a better sense of 'what's going on', they indicate that indigent suspects are oftentimes better off by remaining isolated from these negotiations because there is less opportunity for potentially stigmatizing or discrediting information to be revealed.

Similarly, the findings presented here make Black's (1989) concept of 'the desocialization of law' (or the procedure whereby discrediting social characteristics are essentially sanitized from legal cases) problematic.[26] This is because, as revealed through this study, social situations are *inherent* features of evidence; i.e., one cannot attempt to prove a case without also introducing into evidence such facts as 'who' did what (or perhaps 'could not have done' something) *because of* their social situation.

Nonetheless, there are some alternatives by which reformers might attempt to alleviate the problem of substantive injustice. They range from more to less extreme measures of coercion and change. At one extreme is, of course, the cultivation of class conflict and revolution in the traditional Marxist sense.[27] This would entail, in essence, that the working class acquire a consciousness of common interests and goals, seize power from the elites, and then institute en masse some type of classless social system. Such change implies that the current legal system would either disappear completely or, at the very least, laws would be invoked under more equitable social conditions and in a more equitable social context. In this scenario, for example, either the crime of theft would no longer exist or no single person would be considered any more or less culpable for theft due to his social class. This alternative, however, entails pursuing a generally distasteful strategy of violence, death and destruction that has yet to be proven successful for actualizing the dream of a communist utopia.

At the other extreme is a nonviolent alternative involving attempts to change the social consciousness of persons responsible for judging defendants. As noted by Bellah et al (1985), Americans, especially, tend to view their world and social life in terms of the 'individual'. Success, for example, is typically viewed as individual achievement. However, by attempting to cultivate in persons a consciousness of 'social ecology' (or, a consciousness whereby persons become aware of social inter-relationships), people might learn to relate individuals to the larger society and to recognize the inequities and injustices associated with social class. This could then result not only in a more fair adjudication of criminal cases, but also in the realization of the need for overall social reform and a relatively peaceful social movement that would concentrate on changing the inequitable social conditions that underlie injustice in the legal system.

To some extent, this type of consciousness-raising may be carried-out by attorneys who, in some court jurisdictions, are permitted to conduct their own *voir dires* (i.e., jury selections). In these pre-trial proceedings, the attorneys question jurors in an attempt not only to ascertain whether they will be biased against their cases but also to educate them about the potentially disturbing and/or prejudicial facts they will encounter. With regard to the defendant's social class, it would not be unfeasible for defense attorneys to ask jurors such questions as 'It won't bother you that my client has only a third grade education, will it?' or 'You realize that simply because someone is unemployed and homeless, that doesn't mean they committed robbery, correct?' Whether or not this strategy would actually work is unclear. Nevertheless, defense attorneys who are committed to protecting their lower-class clients' interests may find that it is at least worth the effort because it *could* work.

Between the two extremes is the strategy of using the law itself to litigate social injustice and thereby attempting to compel more equitable social conditions on a case-by-case basis. As some observers have noted,[28] law encompasses a number of vaguenesses or cultural contradictions whereby actors are oftentimes able to negotiate or legitimate more preferable social realities. As we have seen in this study, one important legal document in this respect is the U.S. Constitution. By employing this document, we might attempt, for example, to litigate and thereby institute 'equal opportunity' to the greatest extent possible (e.g., equal educational opportunity, equal occupational opportunity, etc.). By doing so successfully, the powerless would then ultimately be provided with the same opportunities and access to resources as the powerful and overall social equality and justice would prevail.

In conclusion, it is important to state here that there are no guarantees that any of the alternatives for social reform discussed above will actually prevail. Indeed, one might reasonably argue that the chance of triumph in any scenario is minimal at best. Yet it is indisputable that doing nothing will accomplish nothing. Only by taking action are we increasing the probability of achieving justice.

Notes

1   See for example, Blumberg (1967b), Sudnow 1967) and Swigert and Farrell (1977).
2   This term has been used by other researchers including Lind and Tyler (1988), Paternoster et al (1997), Tyler (1988) and Tyler and McGraw (1986). Its meaning as intended here derives from that associated with Weber's (1968) concept of 'formal rationality' and Nonet and Selznick's (1978) concept of 'autonomous law'.
3   Malcolm Feeley (1979) first used the term 'substantive justice' to characterize the 'fairness' of settling cases in light of the extra-legal burdens that trials put on defendants. Similarly, the term 'substantive injustice' here refers to the inequitable extra-legal circumstances under which the law is invoked. The meaning is derived from Weber's (1968) concept of 'substantive rationality' and Nonet and Selznick's (1978) concept of 'responsive law'.
4   The Defenders' everyday stance toward law might also be characterized as 'with the law'.

As described by Ewick and Silbey, being 'with the law' is a form of legal consciousness whereby

> ... law is described and 'played' as a game, a bounded arena in which preexisting rules can be deployed and new rules invented to serve the widest range of interests and values. It is an arena of competitive tactical maneuvering where the pursuit of self interest is expected and the skillful and resourceful can make strategic gains (1998: 48).

5   See also the findings of Heumann (1975), Mather (1979), McDonald (1985), Neubauer (1974) and Rosett and Cressey (1976) concerning the behavior of other defense attorneys.

6   See also the findings of Heumann (1975), and Mather (1979).

7   See also Flemming (1986).

8   In their study entitled 'Societal Reaction to Deviants: The Case of Criminal Defendants', Bernstein et al maintain that interactionist research '... should probe deeper into reactor held values to determine what values are held, and when they become salient determinants of societal responses (1977: 381)'. This research has fulfilled these demands in the manner described below.

9   C.f., Wiseman (1979).

10 See also Frohmann (1991) and Stanko (1982).

11 See Walker, Spohn and Delone (1996) for an overview of these rates in conjunction with related crime statistics.

12 Among those who report at least some findings consistent with those reported here are Clarke and Koch (1976), Cooney (1994), Farrell (1971), Hagan (1974), Jankovic (1978), Kalven and Zeisel (1976), Kruttschnitt (1980; 1982), Lizotte (1978), Reskin and Visher (1986) and Swigert and Farrell (1977).

13 See for example, Bernstein et al (1977), Chiricos and Waldo (1975), Clarke and Koch (1976), Eisenstein and Jacob (1977), Hagan (1974), Holmes et al (1987), Myers (1980) and Willick et al (1975).

14 See Kruttschnitt (1980) for an exception to this tendency.

15 Among those who have controlled for such legal variables as 'prior record' and 'strength of the evidence' are Clarke and Koch (1976), Holmes et al (1987), Kruttschnitt (1980), Myers (1980), Reskin and Visher (1986), Swigert and Farrell (1977) and Willick et al (1975).

16 See for example, Myers (1980).

17 See for example, 'Effective Assistance of Counsel for the Indigent Criminal Defendant: Has the Promise Been Fulfilled?' (1986).

18 See for example, Feeley (1986), Hermann et al (1977), Skolnick (1967), Wheeler and Wheeler (1980) and Wice (1985).

19 See Lorenz (1986) and Emmelman (1993).

20 A Trustee position was a voluntary, unsalaried position. Trustees either nominated themselves or were nominated by others for their positions. Earlier in the history of Defense Alliance, the President of the County Bar Association appointed all twelve members of the Board to their positions. Later, the number of Trustees increased to fifteen and the County Bar Association appointed only five. The other ten were appointed by the County Board of Supervisors. This change occurred as Defense Alliance increased its share over the indigent caseload in the county. As will be noted later in this discussion, however, the significance

of this shift appears to have something to do *not* with Defense Alliance's increase in size per set but instead with its increase in power and (as McIntyre notes) its subsequent ability to challenge the legitimacy of other court actors' behaviors. That is, by putting more political appointees on the Board, the County Board of Supervisors believed it was better able to channel political dictates through Defense Alliance.

21 See for example, Powell (1985).
22 The County Board of Supervisors as well as the District Attorney's Office alleged that the Director of Defense Alliance had once contributed to a prison escape and was therefore ethically unqualified for the position he was about to assume. However, upon hearing the allegations, the Director promptly resigned his position. Nevertheless, instead of opting to hire another Director, the Supervisors decided to establish a public Defender system.
23 Both Blumberg's (1967b) and Alschuler's (1975) findings indicate that with private attorneys especially, clients 'get what they pay for'. Since the poor receive free services from attorneys who typically care about their needs and since the wealthy can afford a great deal of legal service, it is easy to conclude that it is actually the working and middle classes who are most apt to suffer from low quality legal service.
24 See for example, Chambliss and Seidman (1982), Nonet and Selznick (1978), Reiman (1998), and Weber (1968).
25 E.g., Alschuler (1975) and Mather (1979).
26 C.f., Cotterell (1991).
27 See for example, Marx (1968).
28 See, for example, Amsterdam and Bruner (2000), Bannister and Milovanovic (1990), Ewick and Silbey (1998), McIntyre (1987), Sarat and Kearns (1998a; 1998c) and Silbey (1992).

Bibliography

Albonetti, C.A. (1992), 'Charge Reduction: An Analysis of Prosecutorial Discretion in Burglary and Robbery Cases', *Journal of Quantitative Criminology,* vol. 8, pp. 317–333.

Alschuler, A.W. (1968), 'The Prosecutor's Role in Plea Bargaining', *University of Chicago Law Review*, vol. 36, no. 1, pp. 50–112.

Alschuler (1975), 'The Defense Attorney's Role in Plea Bargaining', *The Yale Law Journal*, vol. 84, no. 6, pp. 1179–1314.

Alschuler (1986), 'Personal Failure, Institutional Failure, and the Sixth Amendment', (Effective Assistance of Counsel for the Indigent Criminal Defendant: Has the Promise Been Fulfilled? New York University, March 23, 1985.) *Review of Law and Social Change;* vol. 14, 1, pp. 149–156.

American Bar Association (1986), *Standards for Criminal Justice,* second edition. Boston: Little, Brown and Company.

Amsterdam, Anthony G. and Jerome Bruner. (2000), *Minding the Law*. Cambridge, Massachusetts: Harvard University Press.

Aprile, J. Vincent II. (1986), 'A Response', (Effective Assistance of Counsel for the Indigent Criminal Defendant: Has the Promise Been Fulfilled? New York University, March 23, 1985.) *Review of Law and Social Change*; vol. 14, 1, pp. 47–50.

Balbus, Isaac. (1973), *The Dialectics of Legal Repression: Black Rebels before the American Criminal Courts*. New York: Russell Sage Foundation.

Bannister, Shelley and Dragan Milovanovic. (1990), 'The Necessity Defense, Substantive Justice and Oppositional Linguistic Praxis', *International Journal of the Sociology of Law*, vol. 18, no. 2, pp. 179–198.

Beirne, Piers and James Messerschmidt. (1995), *Criminology*, second edition. Orlando, Florida: Harcourt Brace College Publishers.

Beirne, Piers and Richard Quinney (eds). (1982), *Marxism and Law*. New York: John Wiley and Sons.

Bellah, Robert N., Richard Madsen, William M. Sullivan, Ann Swidler, and Steven M. Tipton. (1985), *Habits of the Heart*. San Francisco: Harper and Row, Publishers.

Berger, Peter L. and Thomas Luckmann. (1967), *The Social Construction of Reality*. New York: Doubleday and Co., Inc.

Bernstein, Ilene Nagel, William R. Kelly, and Patricia A. Doyle. (1977), 'Charge Reduction: An Intermediary Stage in the Process of Labeling Criminal Deviants', *Social Forces,* vol. 56, no. 2, pp. 362–384.

Black, Donald. (1989), *Sociological Justice*. New York: Oxford University Press.

Black, Donald. (1993), *The Social Structure of Right and Wrong*. San Diego: Academic Press

Black, Henry Campbell. (1968), *Black's Law Dictionary*. Revised 4th edition by the publisher's editorial staff. St. Paul, Minn.: West Publishing Co.

Blumberg, Abraham. (1967a), *Criminal Justice*. Chicago: Quadrangle Books.

Blumberg (1967b), 'The Practice of Law as a Confidence Game: Organizational Cooptation of a Profession', *Law and Society Review,* vol. 1, no. 2, pp. 15–40.

Blumer, Herbert. (1978), 'Society as Symbolic Interaction', in *Symbolic Interaction*, Jerome G. Manis and Bernard N. Meltzer, eds, pp. 97–103. Boston: Allyn and Bacon, Inc.

Brannigan, Augustine and Michael Lynch. (1987), 'On Bearing False Witness: Credibility as an Interactional Accomplishment', *Journal of Contemporary Ethnography* vol. 16, no. 2, pp. 115–146.

Burke, Kenneth. (1989), *The Heritage of Sociology: Kenneth Burke on Symbols and Society*, edited and with an introduction by Joseph R. Gusfield, University of Chicago Press: Chicago.

Burke, Kenneth. (1969), *A Grammar of Motives*. Berkeley: University of California Press.

Carlin, Jerome. (1962), 'Lawyers On Their Own: A Study of Individual Practitioners in Chicago', in *Law and The Behavioral Sciences*, Lawrence Friedman and Stewart Macauley (eds). 1977, pp. 944–949. New York: The Bobbs-Merrill Co., Inc.

Carrier, James G. (1982), 'Knowledge, Meaning, and Social Inequality in Kenneth Burke', *American Journal of Sociology*, vol. 88, no. 1, pp. 43–61.

Chambliss, William J. (1964), 'A Sociological Analysis of the Law of Vagrancy', *Social Problems* vol. 12, no. 1, pp. 67–77.

Chambliss, William and Robert Seidman. (1982), *Law, Order, and Power*. Reading, Massachusetts: Addison-Wesley Publishing Co.

Chiricos, Theodore G. and Gordon P. Waldo. (1975), 'Socioeconomic Status and Criminal Sentencing: An Empirical Assessment of a Conflict Proposition', *American Sociological Review*, vol. 40, no. 6, pp. 753–772.

Church, Thomas W. Jr. (1976), 'Plea Bargains, Concessions and the Courts: Analysis of a Quasi-Experiment', *Law and Society Review*, vol. 10, no. 3, pp. 377–401.

Church, Thomas W. Jr. (1982), *Examining Local Legal Culture: Practitioner Attitudes in Four Criminal Courts*. U.S. Dept. of Justice: National Institute of Justice.

Cicourel, Aaron. (1968), *The Social Organization of Juvenile Justice*. New York: Crane, Russak and Company, Inc.

Cicourel, Aaron. (1974), *Cognitive Sociology*. New York: The Free Press.

Clarke, Stevens H. and Gary G. Koch. (1976), 'The Influence of Income and Other Factors on Whether Criminal Defendants Go to Prison', *Law and Society Review*; vol. 11, no. 1, pp. 57–92.

Cloyd, Jerald Wray. (1975), 'The Ideals of Justice and the Practical Organizational Contingencies Affecting Criminal Cases Involving Intoxicants'. Unpublished Dissertation. The University of California, San Diego.

Collins, Randall. (1981), 'Micro-Translation as a Theory-Building Strategy', In *Advances in Social Theory and Methodology*, K. Knorr-Cetina and A.V. Cicourel (eds). Boston: Routledge and Kegan Paul.

Conley, John M. and William M. O'Barr. (1998*), Just Words: Law, Language, and Power*. University of Chicago Press: Chicago

Coombe, Rosemary J. (1998), 'Contingent Articulations: A Critical Cultural Study of Law', in *Law in the Domains of Culture*, Austin Sarat and Thomas Kearns (eds), pp. 21–64. University of Michigan Press: Ann Arbor.

Cooney, Mark. (1994), 'Evidence as Partisanship'. *Law and Society Review*, vol. 28, no. 4, pp. 833–858.

Cotterell, Roger. (1991), 'The Durkheimian Tradition in the Sociology of Law'. *Law and Society Review, vol.* 25, no. 4, pp. 923–945.

Daley, Kathleen. (1987), 'Structure and Practice of Familial-Based Justice in a Criminal Court', *Law and Society Review*, vol. 21, no. 2, pp. 267–290.

Danet, Brend and Bryna Bogoch. (1980), 'Fixed Fight or Free-for-All? An Empirical Study of Combativeness in the Adversary System of Justice', *British Journal of Law and Society*; vol. 7, no. 1, pp. 36–60.

Deosaran, Ramesh. (1984), 'Towards A Social Psychology of Trial by Jury', *British Journal of Criminology*; vol. 24, no. 4, pp. 343–360.

Drechsel, Robert E. (1987), 'Uncertain Dangers: Judges and the News Media', *Judicature,* vol. 70, no. 5, pp. 264–272.

'Effective Assistance of Counsel for the Indigent Criminal Defendant: Has the Promise Been Fulfilled?' (New York University, March 23, 1985.) *Review of Law and Social Change*; vol. 14, no. 1.

Eisenstein, James, Roy B. Flemming, and Peter F. Nardulli (1988), *The Contours of Justice: Communities and Their Courts.* Boston: Little, Brown, and Company.

Eisenstein, James and Herbert Jacob. (1977), *Felony Justice.* Boston: Little, Brown and Company.

Emerson, Robert M. and Blair Paley. (1992), 'Organizational Horizons and Complaint-Filing', in *The Uses of Discretion*, K. Hawkins (ed.). New York: Oxford University Press.

Emmelman, Debra S. (1993), 'Organizational Conditions that Facilitate an Ethical Defense Posture Among Attorneys for the Poor: Observations of a Private Nonprofit Corporation', *Criminal Justice Review* vol. 18, no. 2, pp. 221–235.

Emmelman, Debra S. (1996), 'Trial by Plea Bargain: Case Settlement as a Product of Recursive Decisionmaking', *Law and Society Review* vol. 30, no. 2, pp. 335–360.

Erlanger, Howard S. (1978), 'Lawyers and Neighborhood Legal Services: Social Background and the Impetus for Reform', *Law and Society Review*, vol. 12, no. 2, pp. 253–274.

Ewick, Patricia and Susan S. Silbey. (1998), *The Common Place of Law: Stories from Everyday Life.* The University of Chicago Press: Chicago.

Ewick, Patricia and Susan S Silbey. (1995), 'Subversive Stories And Hegemonic Tales: Toward A Sociology Of Narrative', *Law and Society Review*, vol. 29, no.2, pp. 197–227.

Farr, Kathryn Ann (1984), 'Administration and Justice', *Criminology* vol. 22, no. 3, pp. 291–319.

Farrell, Ronald A. (1971), 'Class Linkages of Legal Treatment of Homosexuals', *Criminology,* vol. 9, May, 49–68.

Feeley, Malcolm (1973), 'Two Models of the Criminal Justice system: An Organizational Perspective', *Law and Society Review*, vol. 7, no. 3, pp. 407–425.

Feeley, Malcolm (1979), *The Process is the Punishment.* New York: The Russel Sage Foundation.

Feeley, Malcolm (1986), 'Bench Trials, Adversariness, and Plea Bargaining: A Comment on Schulhofer's Plan', (Effective Assistance of Counsel for the Indigent Criminal Defendant: Has the Promise Been Fulfilled? New York University, March 23, 1985.) *Review of Law and Social Change*; vol. 14, no. 1, pp. 173–178.

Feild, Hubert S. (1978), 'Juror Background Characteristics and Attitudes toward Rape: Correlates of Jurors' Decisions in Rape Trials', *Law and Human Behavior*; vol. 2, no. 2, pp. 73–93.

Flemming, Roy B. (1986), 'Client Games: Defense Attorney Perspectives on Their Relations with Criminal Clients', *American Bar Foundation Research Journal*, vol. 2, pp. 253–277.

Frohmann, Lisa. (1991), 'Discrediting Victims' Allegations of Sexual Assault: Prosecutorial Accounts of Case Rejections', *Social Problems*, vol. 38, no. 2, pp. 213–226.

Frohmann, Lisa. (1997), 'Convictability and Discordant Locales: Reproducing Race, Class, and Gender Ideologies in Prosecutorial Decisionmaking', *Law and Society Review*, vol. 31, no. 3, pp. 531–556.

Garfinkle, Harold. (1967), *Studies in Ethnomethodology.* Englewood Cliffs: Prentice-Hall, Inc.

Geertz, Clifford. (1983), *Local Knowledge: Further Essays in Interpretive Anthropology*. New York: Basic Books, Inc.

Glaser, Barney and Anselm Strauss. (1967), *The Discovery of Grounded Theory*. Chicago: Aldine Publishing Co.

Glenn, Brian J. (2000), 'The Shifting Rhetoric of Insurance Denial', *Law and Society Review*, vol. 34, no. 3, pp. 779–808.

Goffman, Erving. (1959), *The Presentation of Self in Everyday Life*. New York: Doubleday and Company, Inc.

Goffman, Erving. (1963), *Stigma*. Englewood Cliffs, New Jersey: Prentice-Hall, Inc.

Guggenheim, Martin. (1986), 'Divided Loyalties: Musings on Some Ethical Dilemmas for the Institutional Criminal Defense Attorney', (Effective Assistance of Counsel for the Indigent Criminal Defendant: Has the Promise Been Fulfilled? New York University, March 23, 1985.) *Review of Law and Social Change*; vol. 14, no. 1, pp. 13–21.

Gusfield, Joseph R. (1981), *The Culture of Public Problems*. Chicago: The University of Chicago Press.

Gusfield, Joseph R (1989), 'Introduction' in *The Heritage of Sociology: Kenneth Burke on Symbols and Society*, Kenneth Burke. University of Chicago Press: Chicago.

Hagan, John. (1974), 'Extra-Legal Attributes and Criminal Sentencing: An Assessment of a Sociological Viewpoint', *Law and Society Review*, vol. 8, pp. 357–383.

Hall, Donald. (1975), 'The Role of the Victim in the Prosecution and Disposition of a Criminal Case', *Vanderbilt Law Review* vol. 28, pp. 931–985.

Hall, Jerome. (1952), *Theft, Law, and Society*, Second Edition. Indianapolis, IN: Bobbs-Merrill.

Harris, Marvin. (1999), *Theories of Culture in Postmodern Times*. Walnut Creek, California: AltaMira Press.

Harris, Ronald A. and J. Fred Springer (1984), 'Plea Bargaining as a Game: An Empirical Analysis of Negotiated Sentencing Decisions', *Policy Studies Review*, vol. 4, no. 2, pp. 245–248.

Hay, Douglas. (1975), 'Property, Authority and the Criminal Law', in *Albion's Fatal Tree: Crime and Society in Eighteenth-Century England,* Douglas Hay, Peter Linebaugh, John G. Rule, E.P. Thompson, and Cal Winslow (eds). New York: Pantheon Books.

Hay, Douglas, Peter Linebaugh, John G. Rule, E.P. Thompson, and Cal Winslow (eds), (1975), *Albion's Fatal Tree: Crime and Society in Eighteenth-Century England*. New York: Pantheon Books.

Hays, Sharon. (2000), 'Constructing the Centrality of Culture – and Deconstructing Sociology?' *Contemporary Sociology*, vol. 29, no. 4, pp. 594–601.

Hermann, Robert, Eric Single, and John Boston. (1977), *Counsel for the Poor*. Lexington, Massachusetts: Lexington Books.

Heumann, Milton. (1975), 'A Note on Plea Bargaining and Case Pressure', *Law and Society Review*; vol. 9, no. 3, pp. 515–528.

Heumann, Milton. (1979), 'Thinking About Plea Bargaining' in *The Study of Criminal Courts: Political Perspectives,* Peter F. Nardulli, ed. Cambridge, Massachusetts: Ballinger Publishing Co.

Holmes, Malcolm D., Howard C. Daudistel, and Ronald A Farrell. (1987), 'Determinants of Charge Reductions and Final Dispositions in Cases of Burglary and Robbery', *Journal of Research in Crime and Delinquency*, vol. 24, no. 3, pp. 233–254.

Holstein, James A. (1993), *Court Ordered Insanity*. New York: Aldine De Gruyter.

Homant, Robert J. and Daniel B. Kennedy. (1985), 'Determinants of Expert Witnesses' Opinions in Insanity Defense Cases', *In Courts and Criminal Justice: Emerging Issues*, Susette M. Talarico, ed., pp. 57–59. Beverly Hills: Sage Publications.

Irons, Peter. (1983), *Justice at War*. New York: Oxford Univerity Press.

Jankovic, Ivan. (1978), 'Social Class and Criminal Sentencing', *Crime and Social Justice*, vol. 10, Fall-Winter, pp. 9–16.

Jeffery, C. Ray. (1957), 'The Development of Crime in Early English Society', *The Journal of Criminal Law, Criminology, and Police Science*, vol. 47, no. 6, pp. 647–666.

Johnson, Sheri Lynn. (1985), 'Black Innocence and The White Jury', *Michigan Law Review*; vol. 83, no. 7, pp. 1611–1708.

Kalven, Harry Jr. and Hans Zeisel. (1976), *The American Jury*. Chicago: The University of Chicago Press.

Katz, Jack. (1982), *Poor People's Lawyers in Transition*. New Brunswick: Rutgers University Press.

Kingsnorth, Rodney and Michael Jungsten (1988), 'Driving under the Influence: The Impact of Legislative Reform on Court Sentencing Practices', *Crime and Delinquency*, vol. 34, no. 1, pp. 3–28.

Knorr-Cetine, Karin and Aaron V. Cicourel. (1982), *Advances in Social Theory and Methodology*. Boston: Routledge and Kegan Paul.

Kruttschnitt, Candace. (1980), 'Social Status and Sentences of Female Offenders'. *Law and Society Review*, vol. 15, no. 2, pp. 247–265.

Kruttschnitt, Candace. (1982), 'Respectable Women and the Law', *Sociological Quarterly*, vol. 23, no. 2, pp. 221–234.

LaFree, Gary D. (1985a), 'Adversarial and Nonadversarial Justice: A Comparison of Guilty Pleas and Trials', *Criminology*, vol. 23, no. 2, pp. 289–312.

LaFree, Gary D. (1985b), 'Official Reactions to Hispanic Defendants in the Southwest', *Journal of Research in Crime and Delinquency*; vol. 22, no. 3, pp. 213–237.

Lerner, Benjamin. (1986), 'A Response', (Effective Assistance of Counsel for the Indigent Defendant: Has the Promise Been Fulfilled? New York University, March 23, 1985.) *Review of Law and Social Change*; vol. 14, no. 1, pp. 101–104.

Lester, Marilyn and Stuart C. Hadden. (1980), 'Ethnomethodology and Grounded Theory Methodology: An Integration of Perspective and Method', *Urban Life*; vol. 9, no. 1, pp. 3–33.

Lind, E. Allan and Tom R. Tyler. (1988), *The Social Psychology of Procedural Justice*. New York and London: Plenum Press.

Lizotte, Alan J. (1978), 'Extra-Legal Factors in Chicago's Criminal Courts: Testing the Conflict Model of Criminal Justice', *Social Problems*, vol. 25, no. 5, pp. 564–580.

Loeske, Donileen R. (1992), *The Battered Woman and Shelters: The Social Construction of Wife Abuse*. New York: State University of New York Press.

Lorenz, James, Chairman of the Commission. (1986), 'To Provide Effective Assistance of Counsel', A Report of the Blue Ribbon Commission on Indigent Defense Services to the _____ County Board of Supervisors.

Manis, Jerome G. and Bernard N. Meltzer (eds). (1978), *Symbolic Interaction*. Boston: Allyn and Bacon, Inc.

Maroules, Nicholas. (1986), 'The Social Organization of Sentencing in Alaska's Superior Court', Unpublished Dissertation. University of California, San Diego.

Mather, Lynn M. (1979), *Plea Bargaining or Trial*? Lexington, Massachusetts.: Lexington Books.

Marx, Karl. (1968), *Marxist Social Thought*, edited and with introductory notes by Robert Freedman., introduction by Jerome Balmuth. New York: Harcourt, Brace, Jovanovich.

Matoesian, Gregory M. (1995), 'Language, Law, and Society: Policy Implications of the Kennedy Smith Rape Trial', *Law and Society Review*, vol. 29, no. 4, pp. 669–701.

Maynard, Douglas W. (1982), 'Person Descriptions in Plea Bargaining'. *Semiotica*, vol. 42, no. 2/4, pp. 95–213.

Maynard, Douglas W. (1984a), *Inside Plea Bargaining*. New York: Plenum Press.

Maynard, Douglas W. (1984b), 'The Structure of Discourse in Misdemeanor Plea Bargaining', *Law and Society Review*, vol. 18, no. 1, pp. 75–104.

Maynard, Douglas, W. (1988), 'Narratives and Narrative Structure in Plea Bargaining', *Law and Society Review*, vol. 22, no. 3, pp. 449–481.

McConville, Michael. (1986), 'Dilemmas in New Models for Indigent Defense', (Effective Assistance of Counsel for the Indigent Defendant: Has the Promise Been Fulfilled? New York University, March 23, 1985.) *Review of Law and Social Change*; vol. 14, no. 1, pp. 179–186.

McConville, Michael and Chester L. Mirsky (1990), 'Understanding Defense of the Poor in State Courts: The Sociolegal Context of Nonadversarial Advocacy', *Studies in Law, Politics, and Society*, vol. 10, pp. 217–242.

McDonald, William F. (1979), 'From Plea Negotiation to Coercive Justice: Notes on the Respecification of a Concept', *Law and Society Review,* vol. 13, no. 2, pp. 385–392.

McDonald, William F. (1985), *Plea Bargaining: Critical Issues and Common Practices*. Washington, D.C.: U.S. Dept. of Justice.

McIntyre, Lisa J. (1987), *The Public Defender*. Chicago: The University of Chicago Press.

Mehan, Hugh and Houston Wood. (1975), *The Reality of Ethnomethodology*. New York: John Wiley and Sons, Inc.

Mileski, Maureen. (1971), 'Courtroom Encounters: An Observation Study of a Lower Criminal Court', *Law and Society Review*, vol. 5, no. 4, pp. 473–538.

Miller, Frank. (1970), *Prosecution: The Decision to Charge a Suspect with a Crime*. Boston: Little Brown.

Myers, Martha A. (1979), 'Rule Departures and Making Law: Juries and Their Verdicts', *Law and Society Review*.

Myers, Martha A. (1980), 'Personal and Situational Contingencies in the Processing of Convicted Felons', *Sociological Inquiry*, vol. 50, no. 1, pp. 65–74.

Myers, Martha A. (1987), 'Economic Inequality and Discrimination in Sentencing', *Social Forces*, vol. 65, no. 3, pp.746–767.

Myers, Martha A. and John Hagan. (1979), 'Private and Public Troubles: Prosecutors and the Allocation of Resources', *Social Problems*, vol. 26, no. 4, pp. 439–451.

Nardulli, Peter F. (Ed.). (1979), *The Study of Criminal Courts: Political Perspectives*. Cambridge, Massachusetts: Ballinger Publishing Co.

Nelson, Meredith Anne (1988), 'Quality Control for Indigent Defense Contracts', *California Law Review,* vol. 76, no. 5, pp. 1147–1183.

Neubauer, David W. (1974), *Criminal Justice In Middle America*. Morristown, New Jersey: General Learning Press.

Neuhard, Jim. (1986), 'Free Counsel: A Right, Not a Charity', (Effective Assistance of Counsel for the Indigent Defendant: Has the Promise Been Fulfilled? New York University, March 23, 1985.) *Review of Law and Social Change*, vol. 14, no. 1, pp. 109–118.

Nielsen, Laura Beth. (2000), 'Situation Legal Consciousness: Experiences and Attitudes of Ordinary Citizens about Law and Street Harassment', *Law and Society Review*, vol. 34, no. 4, pp. 1055.

Nonet, Philippe and Philip Selznick. (1978), *Law and Society in Transition*. New York: Harper and Row, Publishers.

O'Barr, William M. (1982), *Linguistic Evidence: Language, Power and Strategy in the Courtroom*. New York: Academic Press.

Padgett, John F. (1990), 'Plea Bargaining and Prohibition in the Federal Courts, 1908–1934', *Law and Society Review*, vol. 24, no. 2, pp. 413–450.

Paternoster, Raymond, Ronet Bachman, Robert Brame and Lawrence W. Sherman. (1997), 'Do Fair Procedures Matter? The Effect of Procedural Justice on Spouse Assault', *Law and Society Review*, vol. 31, no. 1, pp. 163–204.

Platt, Anthony and Randi Pollock. (1974), 'Channeling Lawyers: The Careers of Public Defenders', *Issues in Criminology*, vol. 9, no. 1, pp. 1–31.

Pollner, Melvin. (1974), 'Mundane Reasoning'. Philosophy of the Social Sciences, vol. 4, no. 1, pp. 35–54.

Powell, Michael J. (1985), 'Developments in the Regulation of Lawyers: Competing Segments and Market, Client, and Government Controls', *Social Forces*, vol. 64, no. 2, pp. 281–305.

Pritchard, David. (1986), 'Homicide and Bargained Justice: The Agenda-Setting Effect of Crime News on Prosecutors', *Public Opinion Quarterly*, vol. 50, no. 2, pp. 143–159.

Rabinowitz, Martin J. (1985), 'The Child as an Eyewitness: An Overview', *Social Action and the Law*, vol. 11, no. 1, pp. 5–10.

Radelet, Michael L. and Glenn L. Pierce. (1985), 'Race and Prosecutorial Discretion in Homicide Cases', *Law and Society Review*, vol. 19, no. 4, pp. 587–621.

Reiman, Jeffrey H. (1998), *The Rich Get Richer and the Poor Get Prison*. New York: John Wiley and Sons.

Reskin, Barbara F. and Christy A. Visher. (1986), 'The Impacts of Evidence and Extralegal Factors in Juror's Decisions', *Law and Society Review*, vol. 20, no. 3, pp. 423–438.

Reston, James, Jr. (1995), *Galileo*. New York: HarperPerennial.

Rosett, Arthur and Donald Cressey. (1976), *Justice by Consent*. New York: J.B. Lippencott Company.

Ryan, John Paul and James J. Alfini. (1979), 'Trial Judges' Participation in Plea Bargaining: An Empirical Perspective', *Law and Society Review*, vol. 13, no. 2, pp. 479–507.

Sanders, Andrew. (1985), 'Class Bias in Prosecutions', *Howard Journal of Criminal Justice*; vol. 24, no. 3, pp. 176–199.

Sanger, William W. (1974),   *The History of Prostitution*. New York: AMS Press, Inc.

Sarat, Austin and William L. F. Felstiner. (1986), 'Law and Strategy in the Divorce Lawyer's Office', *Law and Society Review*, vol. 20, no. 1, pp. 93–104.

Sarat, Austin and Thomas R. Kearns (eds). (1995a), *Law in Everyday Life*. The University of Michigan Press: Ann Arbor.

Sarat, Austin. (1995b), 'Beyond the Great Divide: Forms of Legal Scholarship and Everyday Life', In *Law in Everyday Life*, Austin Sarat and Thomas Kearns (eds), pp. 21–62. The University of Michigan Press: Ann Arbor.

Sarat, Austin. (1996), *The Rhetoric of Law*. University of Michigan Press: Ann Arbor.

Sarat, Austin. (1998a), *Justice and Injustice in Law and Legal Theory*. University of Michigan Press: Ann Arbor.

Sarat, Austin. (1998b), Law in the Domains of Culture. Ann Arbor: University of Michigan Press.

Sarat, Austin. (1998c), 'The Cultural Lives of Law', in *Law in the Domains of Culture*, Austin Sarat and Thomas Kearns (eds), pp. 1–20. Ann Arbor: University of Michigan Press.

Schutz, Alfred. (1962), *Collected Papers*, Volume I. Nigjoff: The Hague.

Silbey, Susan. (1985), 'Ideals and Practices in the Study of Law', *Legal Studies Forum*, vol. 9, p. 20.

Silbey, Susan. (1992), 'Making a Place for Cultural Analyses of Law', *Law and Social Inquiry*, vol. 17, no. 1, pp. 39–48.

Skolnick, Jerome H. (1967), 'Social Control in the Adversary System', *Journal of Conflict Resolution*, Vol. 11, no. 1, pp. 52–70.

Stanko, Elizabeth A. (1982), 'The Impact of Victim Assessment on Prosecutors' Screening Decisions: The Case of the New York County District Attorney's Office'. *Law and Society Review*, vol. 16, no. 2, pp. 225–239.

Sudnow, David. (1965), 'Normal Crimes: Sociological Features of the Penal Code in a Public Defender Office', *Social Problems*; vol. 2, no. 3, pp. 255–275.

Swigert, Victoria Lynn and Ronald A. Farrell. (1977), 'Normal Homicides and the Law', *American Sociological Review*, vol. 42, no. 1, pp. 16–32.

Swingewood, Alan. (1998), *Cultural Theory and the Problem of Modernity*. New York: St. Martin's Press.

Talarico, Susette M. (1985), *Courts and Criminal Justice: Emerging Issues*. Beverly Hills: Sage Publications.

Thompson, E.P. (1975), *Whigs and Hunters: The Origin of the Black Act*. New York: Pantheon Books.

Tyler, Tom R. and Kathleen M. McGraw. (1986), 'Ideology and the Interpretation of Personal Experience: Procedural Justice Political Quiescence', *Journal of Social Issues*, vol. 42, no. 2, pp. 115–128.

Tyler, Tom R. (1988), 'What is Procedural Justice? Criteria Used by Citizens to Assess the Fairness of Legal Procedures', *Law and Society Review*, vol. 22, no. 1, pp. 103–135.

Uhlman, Thomas M and Darlene N. Walker. (1979), 'A Plea is No Bargain: The Impact of Case Disposition on Sentencing', *Social Science Quarterly*, vol. 60, p. 218.

Uhlman, Thomas M and Darlene N. Walker. (1980), 'He Takes Some of My Time; I Take Some of His': An Analysis of Judicial Sentencing Patterns in Jury Cases', *Law and Society Review*, vol. 14, no. 2, pp. 323–341.

Ulmer, Jeffrey T. (1996), 'Court Communities Under Sentencing Guidelines: Dilemmas of Formal Rationality and Sentencing Disparity', *Criminology*, vol. 34, no. 3, pp. 383–408.

Underwood, Barbara. (1986), 'A Response', (Effective Assistance of Counsel for the Indigent Criminal Defendant: Has the Promise Been Fulfilled? New York University, March 23, 1985.) *Review of Law and Social Change*; vol. 14, no. 1, pp. 51–52.

Utz, Pamela J. (1978), *Settling the Facts: Discretion and Negotiating in Criminal Court*. Massachusetts: Lexington Books.

Walker, Samuel, Cassia Spohn and Miriam Delone. (1996), *The Color of Justice: Race, Ethnicity and Crime in America*. Boston: Wadsworth Publishing Co.

Weber, Max. (1958), The Protestant Ethic and the Spirit of Capitalism. Introduction by Anthony Giddens. New York: Charles Scribner's Sons.

Weber, Max. (1968), *On Charisma and Institution Building*, edited and with an introduction by S.N. Eisenstadt. Chicago: University of Chicago Press.

Weber, Max. (1979), From Max Weber: Essays in Sociology, translated, edited and with an introduction by H.H. Gerth and C. Wright Mills. New York: Oxford University Press.

Webster's New Collegiate Dictionary. (1976), Springfield, Massachusetts: G. and C. Merriam Company.

Wheeler, Gerald R. and Carol L. Wheeler. (1980), 'Reflections on Legal Representation of the Economically Disadvantaged: Beyond Assembly Line Justice', *Crime and Delinquency*, vol. 26, no. 3, pp. 319–332.

Wice, Paul B. (1985), *Chaos in the Courthouse*. New York: Praeger Publishers.

Willick, Daniel H., Gretchen Gehlker, and Anita McFarland-Watts. (1975), 'Social Class as a Factor Affecting Judicial Disposition Defendants Charged with Criminal Homosexual Acts', *Criminology*, vol. 13, no. 1, pp. 57–77.

Wiseman, Jacqueline P. (1979), *Stations of the Lost*. Chicago: The University of Chicago Press.

Index